facebook

for Smart People

BECAUSE IT'S NOT JUST FOR DUMMIES ANYMORE

By

Sue Ann Kern

Trademarks:

Facebook is a registered trademark of Facebook Inc.

LinkedIn is a registered trademark of LinkedIn Corporation.

Twitter is a registered trademark of Twitter, Inc.

Google and YouTube are registered trademarks of Google, Inc.

Vimeo is a registered trademark of Vimeo.

Adobe Flash is a registered trademark of Adobe Systems.

Flickr is registered trademarks of Yahoo, Inc.

Plaxo is registered trademarks of Plaxo, Inc.

Many of the designations used by manufacturers and sellers to distinguish their products are claimed as trademarks. Where those designations appear in this book, and Face It Social Media was aware of the trademark claim, the designations appear as requested by the owner of the trademark. All other product names and services identified throughout the book are used in editorial fashion only and for the benefit of such companies with no intention of infringement of the trademark. No such use, or the use of any trade name, is intended to convey endorsement of other affiliation with this book.

2012 Face It Social Media Marketing

Copyright 2012 © by Sue Ann Kern

All rights reserved under International and Pan-American Copyright Conventions.

Published in the United States by Face It Social Media Marketing

Park City, UT 84098

Library of Congress Cataloging-in-Publication

Kern, Sue Ann

Facebook for Smart People

ISBN 978-0-9852343-0-0

Printed in the United States of America

Dedication

To my daughters, Samantha and Jessica,
and to my mother, Margaret.

Thank you for everything you have done to make me
the person I have become. Your love, support, and
belief in me have given me the courage to pursue my
passions and create a wonderful life.

facebook

for Smart People

BECAUSE IT'S NOT JUST FOR DUMMIES ANYMORE

Table of Contents

FORWARD: A Fundamental Change in the Way We Communicate 7

1.0   We Are Social Creatures 10

1.1   The Concept of Social Media Marketing 10

1.2   Embrace Social Media 13

1.3   Dunbar's Number 14

1.4   Privacy in a Web 2.1 World 15

2.0   Why Facebook? 17

3.0   Facebook Profiles, Groups, and Pages 21

3.1   Personal Profiles 21

3.2   Groups 23

3.3   Pages 25

3.4   Summary of Differences 29

4.0   Creating your Facebook Page 31

4.1   Creating Your Profile 31

4.2   Page Type and Category 34

4.3   Get Started 37

5.0   Exploring Your Page 39

5.1   The Page Wall 39

5.2   Admin Panel 41

5.2.1   Manage 42

5.2.2   Using Facebook as *"Personal Profile"* or as *"Page Name"* 42

5.2.3   Build Audience 47

5.2.4   Help 49

5.3   Cover Photo 51

5.4   Edit Page 52

5.4.1   Manage Permissions 52

5.4.2   Your Settings 54

5.4.3   Basic Information_ 55

5.4.4   Profile Picture_ 59

5.4.5   Featured_...64

5.4.6   Resources..66

5.4.7   Manage Admins 69

5.4.8   Apps_..70

5.4.9   Mobile...72

5.4.10   Insights..73

5.4.11   Help 73

5.5   The Blue Bar..74

5.6   Home/News Feed..76

5.7   Accessing Your Page 79

6.0   Posting on your Page 83

6.1   Status..83

6.2   Adding Photos and Videos.....................................84

6.3   Adding Links...86

6.4   Asking Questions..87

6.5   Milestones 88

6.6   Events 89

6.7   Pinning a Post 91

6.8   Highlighting a Post 92

6.9   Changing a Post...92

6.10   Deleting a Post..93

7.0   Engaging Your Fans 95

7.1   EdgeRank 96

7.2   Tips for Posting Compelling Content.....................101

7.2.1 How Often Should You Post? When? 101

7.2.2 Share Relevant, Useful and Timely Information 102

7.2.3 Tagging and Posting on Other Pages....................103

7.2.4 Create Fan Interaction...104

7.2.5 Like, Comment, and Share....................................105

7.2.6 Coordinate Your Marketing Strategies..................106

7.2.7 Keep Business and Pleasure Separate...................107

7.2.8 Contests, Sweepstakes and Giveaways..................108

7.2.9   Other Posting Tips 109

8.0   Insights...111

8.1   User Activity...111

8.2   Page Posts Table..113

8.3   Likes..114

8.4   Reach 114

8.5   Talking About This 117

8.6   Check-Ins..117

8.7   Export Data 118

8.8   Weekly Facebook Page Update....................................119

8.9   What To Do With All This Data?...................................121

9.0   Facebook Ads 123

9.1   Design Your Ad...124

9.2   Targeting...126

9.3   Campaigns, Pricing, and Scheduling............................128

9.4   Review Ad and Place Order...131

9.5   Viewing Your Facebook Ads...132

10.0   Social Media Policy Guidelines....................................133

10.1   Who Has Authority? 134

10.2   How Much Time Is Allowed On Social Media Sites? 134

10.3   Who Handles Complaints?..135

10.4   Separate Business and Personal Profiles.................................134

10.5   Give Credit Where Credit is Due 136

10.6   Do Not Divulge Proprietary Information 137

10.7   Reputation Monitoring..137

10.8   Transparency and Disclosure...138

11.0   Go Forth and Be Social! 141

12.0   Common Facebook Definitions...142

FORWARD

A Fundamental Change in the Way We Communicate

What is this world coming to?

In 1986, I graduated from college with a B.S. in Electrical Engineering. This was before home computers. Actually, it was before many *businesses* had computers. One of my senior programming projects required the used of punch cards. A stack of a few hundred cards, typed out one by one, punched by machine, and then read, one-by-one, by the huge computer in the lab. God forbid I drop the stack!

Upon graduation, I landed a coveted job with a small, select group within the Flight Simulation Department at McDonnell Douglas. Pilots would enter a 40' dome, spray painted silver, climb into a mock cockpit and fly a simulated mission. The projection system consisted of a camera mounted on a dual gimbaled system outside the dome in another room. This camera would traverse a wall about 30' by 100' that could have passed for a 6th grade relief map for a geography class: paper-mache hills, sponge bushes, painted rivers. Based on the pilot's command from the simulator, the camera would "fly" left, right, up and down until it reached the end of the wall. Then, pffffst! It would reset back to the left hand side of the wall and start all over again. There were notches punched out of the paper-mache hills and bits of sponge knocked off when the plane would "crash."

The specific department in which I worked was the Computer Generated Imagery (CGI) Department, assigned the task of replacing this soon-to-be obsolete relief map with computer images. At the time, this was considered a very high-tech department because CGI was in its infancy. (Remember Pong?) It would take weeks to generate a digital image of a basic building. What's more, our team shared a single computer between 5 engineers!

About that time, I was given an answering machine for a Christmas present. I was appalled! How rude! Can you imagine...having the audacity to tell someone who calls you that you aren't there so leave a message and you'll call back soon? It's like saying, "Hi! I have a life and you don't! So leave a message and when I return doing whatever fun or monumental task that I'm doing (and you obviously aren't) I'll call you back." Well, that answering machine soon became commonplace. It was no longer considered rude: it was considered rude NOT to have one! Now, I am taken aback when someone actually answers their phone and I have to *communicate* with them!

Answering machines created a fundamental change in the way we communicate.

In 1991, I purchased my first cell phone. I needed it. After all, I had a sales job that required me to travel and be in the office only on occasion. It was a necessary business tool. I was a Field Applications Engineer, a fancy term for someone who is supposed to know the latest in technology of the day. At least a cell phone made me *look* like I was up on the latest technology. Soon, not only field sales people were buying cell phones, but people who had desk jobs. People who didn't have jobs at all...even stay at home moms! Why on earth would these people need a cell phone when they had a perfectly good land line right on their desk or kitchen counter? A cordless land line at that! I never *dreamed* that cell phones would actually begin to replace land lines, much less that CHILDREN would get cell phones!

Cell phones created a fundamental change in the way we communicate

Likewise with home computers and email. Why would you need a computer at home when you have a perfectly good one at work? And email? What's wrong with writing a letter?

Computers created a fundamental change in the way we communicate.

When I was managing the cosmetic dermatology practice in the mid-1990s, I was approached by a few individuals wanting to design a website for our business. Why in the world would a doctor want a website? Who would ever look on the internet to find a doctor? That's what the Yellow Pages are for!

The internet created a fundamental change in the way we communicate

Each of these examples shows how technology introduces a new standard of living and creates a fundamental change in the way we communicate. Like it or not, technology continues to change and improve (ok, that's an opinion, not a fact) and our behavior is forced to change along with it.

Social media is a direct result of how technology has changed the way we communicate with our friends, family, as well as the way we communicate with companies, brands and celebrities. It has helped reunite childhood friends, birth mothers to the children they set out for adoption, helped improve customer service. It has proven to be a major force in political uprisings. It has been blamed for divorces and murders.

The first time I was aware of this social media phenomenon was in 2006, when Christine Dolce got her 15 minutes of fame as the first person to have 1,000,000 MySpace Friends. MySpace? What in the world is MySpace? Folks, that was not that many years ago.

Today, social media is everywhere and penetrating almost every aspect of our lives. Social media has created a fundamental change in the way we communicate. Like it or not.

Now look what the world has come to.

Welcome to the world of social media.

1.0　We Are Social Creatures

As social creatures, we need interpersonal communication to survive and thrive. Think back to your world history classes and how ancient man created the alphabet, smoke signals, hieroglyphics and such to communicate with each other for protection and posterity. It has been proven that having a strong social network can help you live a longer, happier and healthier life.

But even on a lighter note, we rely on our friends for help in other, less life-threatening situations. How will you find the best restaurant to go to on Saturday night? Chances are, you'll ask your friends. How will you decide on which dealership to buy your new car? Chances are, you'll ask your friends. Businesses use polls, focus groups, and surveys to find out what their customers want. They share coupons and discounts to encourage new clients and reward returning ones.

We have always used social networks to communicate and ask for suggestions, referrals, or help. So, if you think about it, the basic concept behind of social media has been around forever.

1.1　The Concept of Social Media Marketing

Social media marketing is based on the two simple marketing premises:

- Permission-based
- Word-of-mouth.

Permission-based marketing allows us, the customer, to decide with which businesses the want to engage. It gives us the opportunity to give permission to a company to share their information, news, promotions, and advertisements with us. This concept suggests that we should be able to specify which companies we are interested in and want to hear what they have to offer, and we can deny access to those with whom we are not interested.

We are tired of being "advertised at" by companies we have no interest in. We are constantly bombarded with television commercials, radio ads, billboards, emails and direct mail pieces by companies that we couldn't care less about. We have become saturated and jaded. Through social media, we are able to connect with a business that offers a product or service in which we have an interest. If we don't have a baby, we may not be interested in diapers. If we are in the market for a new refrigerator, we *do* want to hear what refrigerator manufacturers and dealers have to say.

Word-of-mouth, as we all know, is the best form of advertising you cannot buy. We are more likely to trust the referral from a friend then we are from a glossy magazine ad or flashy television with a paid celebrity spokesperson or model. When we know a friend or family member has had a good experience with a product of service, the chances are that we will follow their footsteps and recommendations. Besides, it saves us time by taking advantage of their research!

Social media is also about creating a community of brand advocates. Brand advocates are those people who have developed affinity and respect the product and service, and want to share their experience with others. Many of us want to communicate with a particular company to let them know what we like or dislike. We want to recommend these businesses to our friends and family who are interested in the same things. We want to warn them of a bad experience, as well. We want to share our new ideas and suggestions and have a part in product development. We want to be one of the first to hear of their special offers, discounts, or coupons.

We want to utilize social media for a quick response to our customer service needs. Many times, brand advocates are created when a frustrated customer is met with quick and effective customer service, or when someone makes a suggestion to a company and then is thanked or rewarded for their contribution. Social media allows the platform for a constructive dialogue and mutually beneficial relationship between the business and individual.

Social media is here to stay, in some shape or form. You can embrace it or fight it, but you can't ignore it.

1.2   Embrace Social Media

I, for one, am embracing social media. I find it fun, exhilarating, and useful, both professionally and personally. I use sites like Facebook to stay in contact with my friends and family, and especially to connect with others with whom I wouldn't have the time to otherwise. I enjoy seeing pictures from an old friend's son's graduation. That friend and I like each other, but are not close enough for her to mail (or even email) pictures to me. Social media makes it easier for us to communicate. When a friend shares in interesting link to an article, I'm more likely to read it based on their suggestion rather than a stranger's. Connecting with someone via a professional social site, like LinkedIn, is much more acceptable than cold calling.

I'm sure many of you are fighting social media. You may think it's all about people telling the world about they had for breakfast. You may think that you don't have the time. You may think it will be the ruin of personal communications.

Many people think that social media dilutes the way we communicate.

I think it allows you to communicate with more people than you could without social media.

1.3 Dunbar's Number

British anthropologist, Robin Dunbar, theorized in the 1970s that every individual is physically and temporally limited to the number of personal connections that they can have. This limit is determined by the number of hours it takes to actually keep in touch with the person on a regular basis and maintain a minimal relationship. There are only 24 hours in a day and only so much time you can spend communicating directly with someone. Dunbar's number was never actually quantified, but ranges between 100 and 230, with 150 being the agreed upon number. I think that's pretty accurate. Most people have about 150 friends, family members, and business associates with whom they can keep up regular communications.

Social media, on the other hand, allows you to keep a superficial, yet often sufficiently satisfying, relationship with many others at the same time. One simple post can be seen by countless others, and you are able to see what they post as well. No phone call, no lunch or coffee meeting. Now granted, you wouldn't sacrifice your top 150 and communicate with them only through social media, but now you can open up your network to many others who didn't make the cut but with whom you'd still like to keep in touch.

Let me make it clear that I don't believe that "He who dies with the most Facebook Friends wins." I am not a LION-LinkedIn Open Networker, nor do I follow thousands of people on Twitter. I only connect people I know and want to communicate with. I regularly ignore invitations to connect.

I'm friends with only about 400 people on Facebook. Some of these are good friends and family with whom I get together with or chat on the phone with regularly. They are part of my 150. In addition to the quality time I insist on spending with them, we still send messages and photos to each other on social media. That adds to our relationship rather than distracts from it.

The remaining Friends are people with whom I wouldn't be able to spend the time to keep a relationship going, but with whom I would like to keep in touch. Some are from my high school or college who didn't make my 150 cut, but, thanks to social media, have developed a newfound friendship! At my last reunion, we may have engaged in superficial small talk. At our next reunion, we'll probably meet for coffee or cocktails and ask each other about the vacation pictures we shared on Facebook.

So, by all means, enjoy your 150. Spend quality time with them. Send them old fashioned letters or new fangled emails. But allow social media to open up your sphere of influence beyond your 150 and cause a fundamental change in the way you communicate.

1.4   Privacy in a Web 2.1 World

Another complaint about social media is privacy. People are scared that others will find out things about them that they do not want them to know. The solution is so simple! Check your privacy settings and do not post anything that you don't want your grandmother to know!

Privacy invasions can happen with an old-fashioned mail or email. If you send a letter or an email with content that others may find offensive, there is no guarantee that that letter or email won't find its way to those same people who may be offended. Once the letter or email is sent, it is out of your hands. So be aware and be careful. If something is private, don't write about it to anyone!

A woman at one of my recent workshops stated that Facebook is now a major cause of divorce, because people find out on the site about their

significant other having an affair. I looked at her incredulously, and a bit pathetically and replied, "Don't you think that the major cause for a divorce is a bad marriage?" The affair wouldn't happen if the marriage was not having problems, but that's subject matter for another book. The fact that they would have posted something incriminating on the internet in general is just sheer stupidity. But the fault is not with Facebook. The fault is with their lack of integrity and scruples! Or, of course, their spouse.

So go ahead and have fun with social media. Who knows? Maybe you'll reacquaint with your old high school or college sweetheart. Maybe you'll connect with your best friend from grade school. Maybe you'll learn of a perfect job opening that is exactly what you've been hoping for. Just don't post about anything unless you've already told your grandma. Because whatever happens in Vegas, does not stay in Vegas. It stays on Facebook, on Google+, on Twitter, on YouTube, on Plaxo, on Vimeo, on Flickr...

2.0   Why Facebook?

As everyone who gone to the movies recently knows, Facebook started out "innocently enough" as a way for college kids to connect, and to see which coeds were the cutest. But, in this capitalistic society we live in, someone figured out a way to monetize it and use it to sell things to these college kids. Hence, the birth of the Facebook Page for business.

It's only been a short time since people began to research companies on the internet and make their buying decision based on what they found on the company's website, essentially making the Yellow Pages obsolete. Even if the purchase was made at a brick and mortar location rather than online, a web presence helped the consumer confirm their choice. Many studies have shown that a large percentage of products or services purchased instore were first researched online.

A few years ago, if a company did not have a website, and a prospective customer couldn't find them online to research their intended purchase, then the company was considered out-of-date, not in keeping with today's technology and trends, and possibly even unprofessional. If they couldn't keep up with the times and have a website, how could they be depended upon them to provide reliable and up-to-date products and services? How could they compete with other companies who were current with today's technology? The business may have been quite viable, professional, and provide quality products and services, but because they did not have a website, this was not the image they projected.

Today, the same can be said for Facebook. A business without a Facebook Page may seem out of touch and not up-to-date with technology. Facebook has become a vital resource for people to learn about businesses, products and services in which they are interested. Millions of people use Facebook to search information on companies, their products, services, location, reviews, specials, even to make purchases much in the same way they use websites. Some don't even bother to link to a website since most, if not all, of the information they are looking for is found on a company's Facebook Page.

But why Facebook? Out of the hundreds of social media sites to choose from, what has made Facebook so powerful?   Data from The Nielson Company, comScore and Facebook reveals quite compelling information:

- First of all, Facebook has become the #1 internet site, surpassing Google, Yahoo, AOL, and all Microsoft sites. That is no small feat.
- The average Facebook User spends about 7 hours and 46 minutes on the site each month, compared to the next highest most popular site, AOL Media at 2 hours and 53 minutes.
- Facebook has over 845 Million active users around the world as of December 2011, and this number is growing by the minute. Did you know that over 140 Million users log on every day? That's more than 3 times it's closest competitor!
- You may think that this is just for teenagers and college students, but the fact remains that Facebook is the fast growing social media site for those of us who are 35 years and older.
- More than 53% of US marketers monitor their Facebook presence and engagement with users.

One of the reasons Facebook has grown so rapidly and has such a gargantuan user base is the fact that it has become a "one-stop-shop". Once on Facebook, a consumer can get all of the information they want on a company without having to leave the site. They can even use Facebook instead of email, instant messaging and photo sharing sites. Facebook also allows them to filter out the noise created by other businesses and services that are not relevant in their lives at this point in time.

The altruistic purpose of a Facebook Page is to create a community of people who are interested in the services and products that a company provides. As a business owner, your responsibility on your Page is to provide information that makes your client's life easier, more informed, profitable, peaceful, healthy, happier, and fulfilled. Better. Because it is a social network, your Facebook Page provides the opportunity for your customers and prospective clients to not only see what you are doing and offering, but to interact with you and give you valuable feedback. And if that means more sales of your product, then so be it.

Your Fans (those who Like your Page) have the opportunity to ask questions of you and of other people who participate in your Page. They can also give reviews, ideas, comments and even complaints. You, in turn, must take advantage of this and reply to their comments, and quickly act on their complaints and help solve their problems. Remember, people will complain more than they will compliment, so you have a unique opportunity to turn these negatives into a positive and hopefully create a brand ambassador in doing so.

So, although it is important to create a relationship and dialog with your customers on social media, the primary reasons for your business to have a presence on Facebook are to make things convenient for your customers and potential clients...and to expand your business.

Regardless of whether or not you want to participate on Facebook on a personal level, the case has been made to convince you to participate on a professional level. Even if you don't participate, there are over 800,000,000 other Facebook Users around the world, and you can bet many of these are your customers, or should be.

If they are not your customers, they may be your competitors.

3.0 Facebook Profiles, Groups, and Pages

Facebook has developed these three entities for engaging with others users. Each has unique features and attributes, and it is important to understand the basic differences.

3.1 Personal Profiles

A Facebook Personal Profile (Figure 1) is personal account that you use to share personal information, messages, photos, links, and videos with your friends, family and acquaintances.

Every Personal Profile is linked to a unique email address. An email address cannot be used more than once, because Facebook tries to prohibit individuals from having more than one profile. However, there may be many duplicate names for Personal Profiles. You may want to consider using your middle initial or name in your Personal Profile, to differentiate from profiles with the same name.

Your Profile Picture will be linked with your Personal Profile name. Replace the standard avatar with a friendly picture which will make it easy for people to find you. Be creative and have fun with your Profile Picture! This is not the time to be serious with a professional headshot. Save that for LinkedIn.

The people that you choose to connect with on Facebook are called Friends. Facebook Users can search for your profile and send you a Friend request, but no one can connect with you without you accepting that request. You can accept or ignore these requests, as well as block individuals from sending your further requests. And vice versa. Use your privacy settings to limit what Facebook Users who are not your Friends see when they view your Page.

Once the request is accepted, your Personal Profiles are linked and you can communicate with your Friend. Your posts will show up on their News Feed and vice versa (depending on your settings). You can Like, Comment on, and Share posts with your Friends. You can send them personal Messages that won't show up in their News Feed (consider these a Facebook email equivalent) as well as invite them to Events.

Only people (not businesses) are supposed to create Personal Profiles, according to Facebook's Terms of Agreement. If a business, company, or any entity other than an individual creates and uses a Personal Profile to promote their business, and Facebook finds out, they could delete the Profile without warning.

Figure 1: Facebook Personal Profile

Through a Personal Profile, you can Like Facebook Pages. This is what makes Pages such a powerful marketing tool for businesses. Facebook Pages want and need you to Like them, and to post comments, feedback, suggestions, recommendations on their Page. They want you to share their posts with your Friends and spread their message. When your Personal Profile Likes a Page for a business or company, you are giving that Page permission to share the messages that they post, which could then appear on your News Feed, in line with your Friends' posts. In turn, you may be able post a message directly on the Page's Wall (depending on the Page's posting permission settings) and see that message on the Page's News Feed. This is a great way to interact with the business and share feedback and ideas.

Be aware that *your* posts that you create on your own Personal Profile will not show up on the News Feed for the Pages that you Like. So you needn't worry about your personal posts being seen by other people who Like the same Pages that you Like.

You can create unique Username, or Vanity URL for your Personal Profile to use in place of the URL automatically generated. The original URL consists of extraneous numbers and letters and can be dozens of characters long and cumbersome to share with others. You can select a unique Username that is personalized, more concise and easier to share.

Thousands of applications can be found and downloaded onto your Personal Profile to improve your Facebook experience. Many are created by Facebook, while most are created by third-party developers. Most apps are perfectly safe to upload, but there are many that are a bit nefarious and may upload and share your personal information along with that of your Friends. Be sure to research the app before you load it and pay attention to any ratings and reviews.

3.2   Groups

A Facebook Group (Figure 2) is intended to provide a platform for individuals who have the same interests, hobbies, and concerns. Groups are great for clubs and groups of people with whom you want to communicate more directly than through a Page, but have a limit of 5000 members. In Groups, you can send Updates and Create Events, communicate using the Chat feature, and even share documents.

Ad individual who creates a Group is called an Admin (Administrator), but is not anonymous, unlike an Admin for a Page. Everyone who joins the Group can see the Admin, and all posts by the Admin appear from the Admin's Personal Profile rather than from the Group.

The Group doesn't have an identity, per se. Its identity is the collection of members. Therefore, each post is entered by a member rather than by the Group. So, even though a logo or photo can be loaded onto the Group's Settings, that image is not seen when a post is made.

Figure 2: Facebook Group

One difference between a Group and a Page is that, when a post is made on the Group's Wall, it does not get posted on the News Feed of the Group's members. Rather than seeing the posts on their News Feed, Group members will get a Notification on their Personal Profile that someone has posted on the Group's Wall. This supports the more intimate and direct feel of the Group, since you may not want everyone who visits your Profile to see what has been posted by the Group. It's also a bit more cumbersome, as you have to dig a bit deeper to access the updates. Plus, your Facebook inbox may be overwhelmed if the members of the Group post frequently.

When you create a Group, you can choose from one of three types: Secret, Closed, or Open. This is another key differentiator between Facebook Pages and Groups. Facebook Pages are always open to the public, whereas Groups have these options.

- Secret Group: Someone can join by invitation only, and only members of the group can see what is posted. A Secret Group will not show up in a Facebook search.
- Closed Group: Can be found in Facebook search, but only Group members can see what is posted. The Admin for a Closed Group must approve any new requests to join.
- Open Group: Can be found in search and the content can be seen by members and non-members. Anyone can join an Open Group.

An annoying feature of Groups is that members can sign up their Friends as members without their permission. Your Friend may sign you up for a Group that you don't want to join, and then you will have to make the effort to leave the Group.

3.3 Pages

A Facebook Page (Figure 3) is intended for use by organizations, public figures and companies to establish an official presence on Facebook, allowing them to connect with and share information with Facebook Users who are interested in their product or service. Facebook Users can view the Page and post messages on the Page Wall, or they can click the Like button to give permission to the Page to be able to send updates directly to their Personal News Feed.

Figure 3: Facebook Page

In order to create a full-featured Facebook Page, the Page must be created and hosted by the owner of a Personal Profile. Realize that, even if you do create a Personal Profile to host your Facebook Page, you do not have to participate in Facebook on a personal level. You can leave your Personal

Profile alone and never accept Friend Requests or even look at it again. You will use it only to access your Facebook Page.

However, if you absolutely insist that you do not want to have a Facebook Personal Profile, but you do want to have a Page for your Business, you can create a basic account to host what is called a Business Page. The basic account cannot be found in search, cannot send or receive friend requests, and cannot create or develop applications.

Business Pages do not have the same functionality as a Page hosted by a Personal Profile. For instance, the Admin of a Business Page cannot view Personal Profiles of their Fans. (Can you imagine where viewing your Fans' information might be helpful?) We will also be discussing throughout the remainder of the book the concept of using "Facebook as a *Page*" and using "Facebook as *Your Personal Profile*". When you create a basic account and a Business Page, you will always be using "Facebook as a *Page*".

Unlike Profiles or Groups, when a Page is created, there are numerous options for the type and category of entity the Page represents. This helps clarify the Page in search, since Facebook does not require unique names for Pages, Groups or Users. It also determines the template for the Page's Basic Information section.

Facebook has created many features which make Pages ideal for businesses. Whereas Personal Profiles require a two-way acceptance in order to be Friends, anyone can become a Fan, or Like, a Page.

A Page cannot send a request to connect with an individual. Rather, the individual must come to the Page and click the Like button to become a Fan of the Page. Similarly, Pages cannot send messages directly to an individual Fan. This is to prevent spam. You can imagine how full your inbox would be if a Page could send Fan requests and messages! However, Fans can initiate a private message to a Page. The Page can then respond and have a private conversation with that Fan.

Pages can be found in public search, so, even if someone is not on Facebook, if they search your company name, the Page can come up in their search results on Google, Bing, Yahoo, etc. This is a huge reason for having a Facebook presence, especially if your business does not have a website.

Pages can Like other Pages, which, just like with a Personal Profile, gives those Pages the permission to post messages on the Page's News Feed. This is a great way for Pages to increase their visibility and share their messages to more people than just those who Like their own Page. It also allows your Page to use its News Feed to track what's going on with other businesses, clients, and yes, competitors on Facebook.

Pages also they generate Insights. Insights are thorough statistics, which can only be seen by the Admins of the Page, to help analyze how Facebook Users interact with the Page. The Admin can see how many Likes the Page has, how many comments were made and when, how much interaction each post received, how many times the Page has been viewed, and how many times a given posting has been made available on the News Feeds of its Fans. This is just a sampling of the data available to Page Admins through Insights.

The Admin of a Page is anonymous, unless the Admin specifically chooses to be known. Anonymity is an advantage for you if you do not want anyone to know that you administer a Page. It is also an advantage to choose *not* to be anonymous if, say, you *are* your business and you want your Fans to recognize you and learn more about you. If you chose not to be anonymous, your Personal Profile Picture will be shown on the Page and your Fans can click on that and view your Personal Profile, according to the privacy settings you have chosen on your profile.

Whereas Groups have Secret, Closed and Open options to restrict membership, Pages do not. Anyone can join a Page. I once heard this concept compared to the fact that a rock band cannot control who wears its t-shirt. However, a Page can remove, or even ban a Fan who is acting inappropriately on the Page.

Pages can have unique Usernames, making it more professional when you share your Facebook Page in your written marketing material or email signatures.

Hundreds of applications, by Facebook and by third-party developers, are available to enhance the functionality of the Page. Again, these applications should be researched carefully so that you don't inadvertently choose one that is not reliable or even one that shares your Fan information.

3.4   Summary of Differences

	Personal Profile	Groups	Pages
Send Requests to Connect	Y	Y – and can add members	N – but Admins can send invitations
Send Messages to Connections	Y	Y	Y- once initiated by the Fan
Search Engine Indexing	Y	Y	Y
Stream Posts in Timeline	Y	N	Y
Targeted Stream Posts	Y	N	N
Connection limitations	N	5000	N
Membership Restrictions	N/A	Y	N
Insights	N	N	Y
Like Pages	Y	N	Y
Unique Username	Y	N	Y
Applications	Y	N	Y

So you may be thinking, WHEW! What am I getting myself into?

As mentioned before, Groups are more suited for book clubs, networking groups, teams, and folks with like-minded interests. However, for a business, Pages offer more features, flexibility and more professionalism.

So let's get started and create your Page!

4.0   Creating your Facebook Page

Congratulations! You've decided that you are going to create a Facebook Page for your business. You understand that, even if you may not want to participate in Facebook *personally*, it is important for your business to have a presence. According to Polaris Marketing Research, over 75% of Americans agree that a business or brand participating on Facebook indicates that it is interested in hearing what customers have to say.

This chapter will teach you how to *create* your Facebook Page, step-by-step. The subsequent chapters will teach you how to *use* your Facebook Page to promote your business and services, step-by-step.

4.1   Creating Your Profile

Because the intention of this book is to discuss the creation and use of a Facebook Page, we are not going to be talking about using a Facebook Personal Profile. Participating in Facebook at a personal level is something that I do not recommend or encourage, from a professional standpoint. I enjoy using Facebook personally to communicate with my family and friends, but whether or not you want to do that is totally your decision. However, I strongly believe that every business should have a presence on Facebook.

With that in mind, however, the things you will learn in this book will be applicable to and helpful in learning to use your Personal Profile.

If you already have your Facebook Profile, you can skip to Section 4.2.

We will be creating the Personal Profile for the sole purpose of hosting your Page. To create your Profile, go to www.facebook.com, where you will be directed to the Facebook Sign Up Page (Figure 4). If you want to create a

Personal Profile that you use to connect with friends and family for fun, then go ahead and fill out the form and use the email address where you want your notifications sent. If you want, you can create a different email account using Yahoo! or Google that is dedicated solely to your Facebook account.

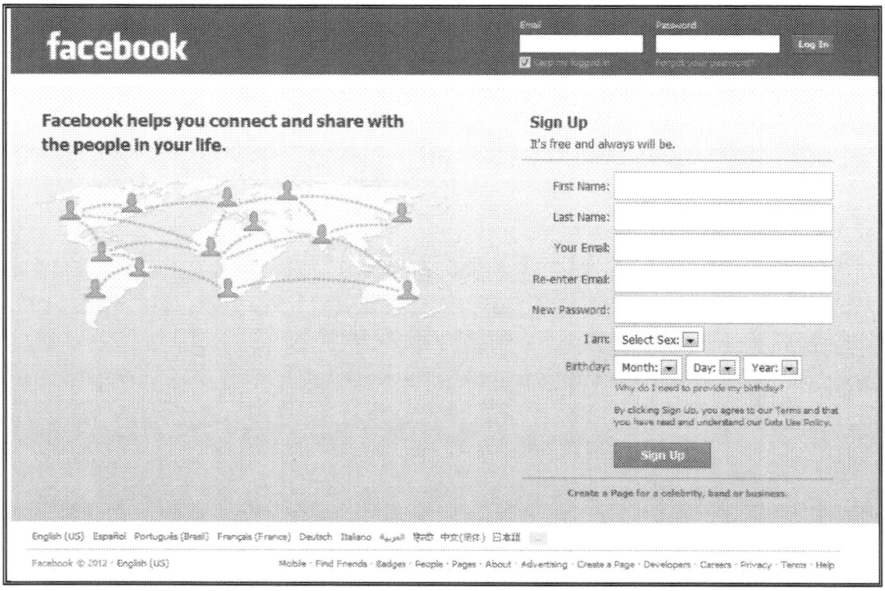

Figure 4: Sign Up Page

If you want to create a Page but do not want to create a Personal Profile, you can click on "Create a Page" below the green "Sign Up" button on the contact form to create a Business Page, as discussed earlier in Section 3.1.3. The information that you provide in this profile will not be available in Facebook search, so you don't have to worry about people finding you and bombarding you with Friend requests. Remember that this type of Business Page does not have the functionality of a Page hosted by a Personal Profile.

Furthermore, throughout this book, we will be talking about "Using Facebook as *Page Name*" and "Using Facebook as *Your Personal Profile*". If you create a Business Page without a Personal Profile, you will always be using "Facebook as *Page Name*".

Facebook requires that you state your birth date, including the year, because you must be 13 or over to have an account. You do not have to show this in your Personal Profile, or you can just show the month and day, so no one needs to know your real age.

Once you have created your Personal Profile, skip through the generic Facebook tutorial and go to the Help option by clicking on the down arrow on the far right side of the blue bar, or by clicking on Help at the bottom of the screen. Type in "How can I create a Page?" Select that topic, look for the word "here" and click on it (Figure 5).

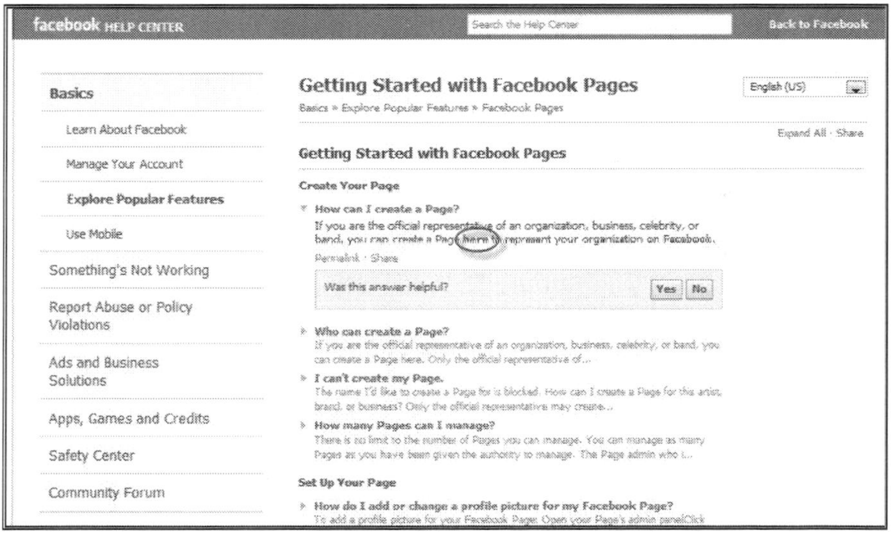

Figure 5: Create Page From Help Center

Or, you can simply scroll to the very bottom of the screen (Figure6). There you will see the following choices. Select "Create a Page."

Facebook © 2012 · English (US)   About · Advertising · Create a Page · Developers · Careers · Privacy · Terms · Help

Figure 6: Create Page From Bottom Of Screen

4.2   Page Type and Category

The next screen that appears will have 6 large boxes representing 6 types of businesses (Figure 7). From these, you will choose one that best describes your business and will help differentiate your Page in Facebook search. These are very generic types, but within each type, you will be able to choose a more specific category.

The Page Type will be chosen from 6 options:

- Local Business or Place
- Company, Organization, or Institution
- Brand or Product
- Artist, Band or Public Figure
- Entertainment
- Cause or Community

Within these six types, there are dozens of category options. One of the purposes of choosing a type and category is for clarity in Facebook search. When someone searches for a word or name, a list of Pages matching that search will appear in a dropdown menu. Under the name of the Page will appear the category.

The other purpose is to determine the template used for the Info section on the Page. While the templates generally don't change drastically, some categories do offer different sections. For instance, a Consulting/Business category will have sections for a Mission Statement and Products, while a Restaurant category has a section for menu prices and payment options.

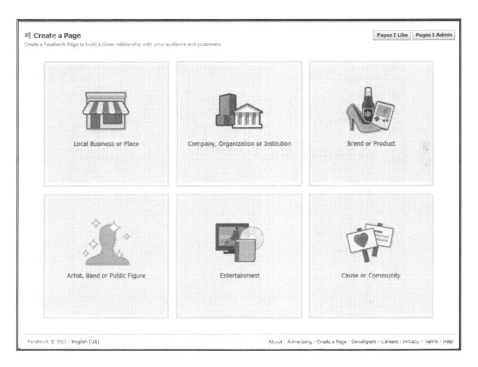

Figure 7: Page Types

Take a few minutes searching Facebook for business types such as yours and see what category they chose. To do this, you will need to back out of the current screen to your Personal Profile and then start entering names in the Facebook Search bar. (Note-you will not be able to do this if you have a Business Account.) Look at the list of Pages that appear in the dropdown menu, and pick a Page – you don't have to Like it to view it. When you are on the Page's landing page, you can click on the Info tab along the left hand side of the screen and see the Info template that is associated with that category. When you find the category that makes sense for your business, and the Info template works for you, then go back and repeat the steps to "Create a Page."

If you choose Cause or Community, this will create a Page that will help you to generate support for your favorite cause, topic, or non-profit organization, but is not really appropriate for a business. You should be able to find the appropriate category and type in the other options, so Cause or Community will only be used if nothing else seems to describe your business.

A Community Page is also automatically created by Facebook when a user enters a unique interest in their profile that does not already have a Page associated with it. Initially, it looks like an excerpt from an online dictionary. If other users find this Community Page and it becomes very popular, with thousands of Fans, it will become adopted a Business Page and maintained by the Facebook community.

Once you have chosen a Category and Type, you are still able to change this in your Facebook Info settings, until you have 100 Fans. So don't spend a lot of time fretting over this. Choose the Page type and category as best you can, and then move on to bigger and better things, like choosing a name for your Page!

Facebook does not require that any names be unique. There can be dozens of Personal Profiles, Groups or Pages with identical names, and finding the entity you are looking for during a search can be infinitely frustrating. For that reason, choose your Page name with some sort of unique flavor. You could use the name of your city or geographic area, or perhaps a title, tagline or award.

4.3   Get Started

At this point, you have chosen your category, the name of your Page, stated your address, clicked on the "I agree to the Facebook Pages Terms", and have clicked on the blue "Get Started" button. Now, Facebook will offer a generic tutorial, or setup wizard, that you can use to guide you through the basics of creating your Page. Each of these steps allows you to "Skip" or "Continue." Everything that the tutorial shows you can be accessed through other areas of your Page, so if you do not want to follow the tutorial, you can bypass this and go to another section of the Page.

For the purposes of this book, we will not be discussing each of the steps in the tutorial. Each of these will be described in detail in later sections. Furthermore, exit your Page at this point and log in later, you will not see the tutorial again.

Note that only the Admin sees this Get Started tutorial. This is a simple tool that Facebook provides to help you set up the most basic constructs of your new Page. The tutorial components vary depending on the category and type that you chose, and you are given the option to skip each step.

When you log Into your Page for the first few times, Facebook will guide you an automatic tour of the Wall. This can be a bit annoying because you have to choose Skip or Next to cycle through each pop-up message that give you a quick description of the various sections. Rest assured that we will be covering each of these topics in this book.

When anyone else visits your Page, they will see your Wall but not the tour. Once your Page has about 25 or 30 Fans, this automatic tour will no longer be displayed.

If you want to view the tour at a later date, you can go to the Admin panel, choose Help, and the select the "Take the Tour" option.

5.0   Exploring your Page

One of the beauties of Facebook is that Pages have standard formats. The layout for every Page, regardless of the type of company or the number of Fans, is the same. All Walls and all News Feeds look the same.

When you access your Page, you will see the "Admin Panel" button, allowing you to access the features and tools available to the Admins. Note that only the Admins can see these options. No one who is visiting your Page will see the Admin Panel or anything that allows them to access the Admin tools for your Page.

5.1   The Page Wall

The Page Wall (Figure 8) contains everything that the Page has posted as well as any direct communication with the Page from other Facebook Users. Think of is as a bulletin board for your office. On that bulletin board, you put your news clips, photos, and other things that you find interesting and that you want to share with others. When someone comes into your office, they may leave you a note on your bulletin board. These notes are messages specifically directed to you, as opposed to a general message for the whole world.

On your Page Wall, everything that you (and the other Admins) post will be displayed, along with any comments on these posts that have been made by your Fans. In addition to these, any posts made directly to your Page from your Fans or from other Pages that you like will also show up on your Wall. When a Fan or another Page tags you or posts a message to your Page, it will show up on your Wall.

Figure 8: The Page Wall

5.2   Admin Panel

Whether you have just created your Page or you are accessing an existing Page that you have already created, you will initially see your Page Wall. In the upper right had corner, below the blue bar, you will see the "Admin Panel" button. Clicking on this button will take you to the inner workings of your Page – the Dashboard, if you will.

The Admin Panel (Figure 9) provides a quick overview of what is going on with your Page. From here, you can view any new messages from Fans, notifications of activity, a list of the most recent Facebook Users who have Liked your Page, and a link to your Insights.

You will also see another set of buttons labeled "Manage", "Build Audience", "Help", and "Hide". The Admin Panel takes up a lot of space on your screen, so when you are done checking out the information shown, click on the "Hide" button to close it.

Figure 9: Admin Panel

5.2.1 Manage

Choosing the "Manage" button allows you to access the "Edit Page" tools for your Page. These tools are discussed in complete detail in Section 5.4.

The "Use Activity Log" shows you to see a list of posts and comments that your Page made, as well as posts and comments that Fans have made on your Page. This is a much easier way to see what has been happening on your Wall in a streamlined fashion, especially if you are looking for a particular post. From here, you can highlight, pin, delete and change the date of any of the posts you've made.

The third option on the Manage button is "See Banned Users". If a Fan is acting inappropriately on your Page and posting spam or unacceptable comments, you, as the Admin, can ban this Fan and prevent them from accessing your Page in the future. You can do this by hovering over the inappropriate post, then clicking on "Report or Ban". You will be given the option delete the post from your Page (it will not be deleted from the user's page or profile) and to ban the user. When you have done this, you will be able to see the list of banned users by clicking on this option.

The option "Use Facebook as ..." lets you to toggle between using "Facebook as *Page Name*" and "Facebook as Your *Personal Profile*". This is a somewhat complicated concept, but must be understood in order to fully utilize the features of your Facebook Page. So let's talk about this now.

5.2.2 Using Facebook as *"Personal Profile"* or as *"Page Name"*

It is important to address the concept of using "Facebook as *Page Name*" or using "Facebook as *Your Personal Profile*." (If you have created a Business Page, this concept is not applicable. However, it will be discussed throughout the book, so you will need to be aware of this feature.)

You can think of this concept as "What is in control of this Facebook session?" Either your Page or your Personal Profile can be in control of the session. For the most part, when you access your Page, you will be able to make any posts and create any events regardless of whether you are using "Facebook as *Page Name*" or as "Facebook as *Your Personal Profile*". There are a few instances when it does make a difference, however.

When you access your Page, you have the choice of using or "Facebook as *Your Personal Profile*" or "Facebook as *Page Name*". If you choose to use "Facebook as *Your Personal Profile*", your Personal Profile is in control of your session.

When your Personal Profile is in control of the session, the blue bar on the top of your screen will be somewhat different from when your Page is in control (Figure 10). The icons on the blue bar will all refer to your Personal Profile, NOT the Page. Following the white "Facebook", you will see an icon that looks like two silhouettes, and icon with two conversation bubbles, and a world icon. If you click on the silhouettes icon, you can view your pending Friend Requests. The conversation bubbles icon will show you any messages you've been involved in, and the world icon will show you Notifications for your Personal Profile.

On the right side of the blue bar, you will see the thumbnail and name of your Personal Profile, the Home button, and a down arrow. Clicking on your Name will take you to your Personal Profile Wall, while clicking on Home will take you to your News Feed.

Clicking on the down arrow will allow you to switch to using Facebook as a Page for any of the Pages that you administer. You can also access account and privacy settings for your Personal Profile, the Help center and Log Out.

When you access your Page while using "Facebook as *Your Personal Profile*", then you can still post status updates, photos, links, videos and questions on your Page. However, you must be aware that tagging will be affected (Section 7.2.3). When you tag another Page in a Post, only those Pages that your Personal Profile Likes can be tagged. You will not have the ability to tag the Pages that your Page Likes.

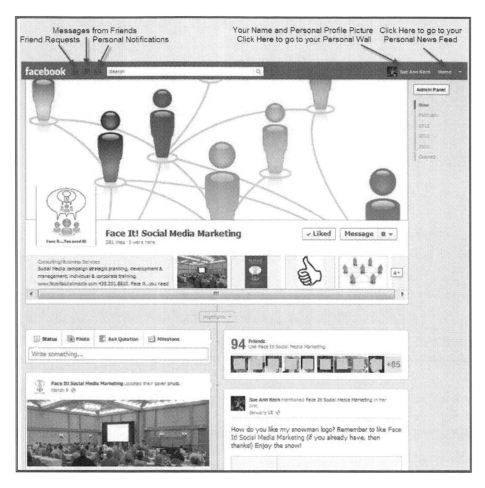

Figure 10: Using "Facebook as *Your Personal Profile*"

Note that when you Personal Profile is in control of your session while you are on your Page, then you only have access to your Page's Wall, but not your Page's News Feed. In order to see the Page's News Feed, you must be using "Facebook as *Page Name*."

When you use "Facebook as *Page Name*", then your Page is in control of your Facebook session, and the properties of the blue bar change. Now, these options refer to the Page, and not your Personal Profile.

You will still see the same icons on the blue bar (Figure 11), but their function changes. If you click on the silhouettes icon, you will view the list of people who Like your Page.

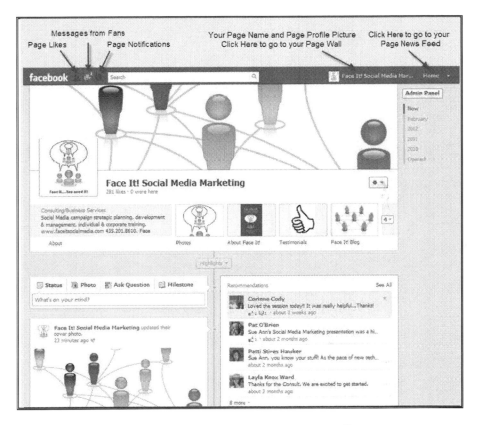

Figure 11: Using "Facebook as *Page Name*"

Clicking on "See All" will allow you to see what other Pages Like your Page, view and change Admins, and to see any Banned Users. The conversation bubbles icon will show you the messages received directly from your Fan. The world icon will show you Notifications for your Page.

On the right side of the blue bar, you will again see the thumbnail and name of your Page, the Home button, and a down arrow. Clicking on your Page's Name will take you to your Page's Wall, while clicking on Home will take you to your Page's News Feed.

When you are using "Facebook as *Page Name*", and you tag another Page in a Post, only those Pages that your Page Likes can be tagged. You will not have the ability to tag the Pages that your Personal Profile Likes.

Furthermore, when you are using "Facebook as *Page Name*" and try to access a 3rd party application or create an ad, then you may get a message directing you to switch to using "Facebook as *Your Personal Profile*" (Figure 12). This may seem like an error message, but it is just a construct within Facebook that requires you use "Facebook as *Your Personal Profile*" in order to do what you want to do.

Figure 12: Using "Facebook as *Page Name*" Warning

There are two ways to toggle between using "Facebook as *Page Name*" and "Facebook as *Your Personal Profile*":

- Click on the downward facing arrow on the far right of the blue bar. You will see the words "Use Facebook as:" and then you can choose to switch back to either your Personal Profile or a different Page.

- When the Admin Panel is displayed, click on the "Manage" button and toggle between your Personal Profile or the Page you are viewing at that time.

Remember that, for the most part, you still have access to most editing and posting functions on your Page regardless if you are using "Facebook as *Your Personal Profile*" or "Facebook as *Page Name*".

As a rule, always use "Facebook as *Page Name*" until you get comfortable with this concept and understand what happens when you switch back and forth.

5.2.3   Build Audience

The second button on the Admin Panel, "Build Audience" offers you ways to help you to publicize your Page to your Facebook Friends, the Facebook community as a whole, and even your connections who are not on Facebook. From here, you can send invitations to Like your Page to the Friends of your Personal Profile as well as to others in your email contact lists. You can also choose to share an invitation to your Page on your personal timeline, and to create an ad to promote to other Facebook Users.

If you choose "Invite Email Contacts", you will be asked to link to your Yahoo, Hotmail, AOL, or other web-based email server or an email client via a .csv (comma separated value) file. Facebook doesn't save your password, but choosing this option will give them access to your email contacts to help them make connections for you. If you have fewer than 5000 contacts, these contacts will be uploaded, and then you can choose to whom you want to send an email or a Facebook message. If the email for your contact is the same for which they have linked to their Personal Profile, then they will see the suggestion for the Page the same way that your Friends would. If not, then they will receive an email inviting them to join Facebook.

Think about this before you do it. First of all, be sure you are on a secure network, as the data that is being transferred is sensitive. But again, do you really want to do this? At this point in time, you'd be hard pressed to find anyone who doesn't know about Facebook. They have probably already received dozens of emails requesting they join Facebook. They may have a Facebook account set up under an email that is different than the one you have in your contact list. You don't know that, so now you are sending them a message to connect on Facebook and they may already be your Friend or a Fan of your Page! The email comes from Facebook with a boilerplate message that is not at all personal. They may resent this and even get mad if they get *one more invitation!* Receiving another may be the straw, and you may just be the one breaking the camel's back.

My suggestion? (I know you want it, or else you wouldn't have bought my book.) Send an email from yourself. This is much more palatable than getting a generic email from Facebook letting your contacts know that you have a Page and you'd appreciate it if they'd take a look and Like it. Entice them by mentioning all of the informative and interesting information that they will receive and how much better their life will be just by becoming a Fan of your Page.

When you choose "Invite Friends...", you will be prompted to select from the Friends of your Personal Profile. Notice that you will only see this option if you are using "Facebook as *Your Personal Profile*". If you are using "Facebook as a *Page Name*", this option will not appear on the drop down menu. Those who you have selected will receive a Message inviting them to Like your Page.

Note that only Page Admins have the option to "Invite Friends..." Fans of a Page cannot do this. This is a relatively new change in the way people who Like a Page can interact and promote a Page. In the past, Fans could send Page Suggestions to their Friends, helping the Page grow organically. Now, when someone Likes a Page, their Friends will see this as in the Ticker on their News Feed. However, the best way for your Fans to help grow your Page is by Sharing, Commenting and Liking the Status Updates.

A point to consider: You definitely want to invite your Friends to Like your Page, but it may not be a good idea to click on the "Invite Friends" button until you have spent some time building your Page. If you send the invitation when you've just created your Page but not yet built it, your Friends will come to your empty Page and find nothing of significance to Like.

It is better to skip this step and then revisit it once you have made several posts, have photos and links and other interesting information that is ready to share and will compel your Friends and contacts to Like the Page.

From the "Build Audience" button, you can also choose "Create An Ad". This is another great way to draw attention to your Page, both from existing Fans and the rest of the Facebook community who have not yet heard of your Page. We will be discussing Facebook Ads in detail in Section 9.0.

5.2.4   Help

The Facebook Help Center is a very comprehensive guide to using Facebook, both from a personal and from a business standpoint. Spend a couple of minutes perusing the Help Center and get a feel for how to search for answers to questions you may have.

If you access the Help Center from your Page, you will be taken to the "Facebook Pages" section automatically. You can also access Help from the down arrow on the right of the blue bar. This will take you to the first page of the Help Center. To access the help for Pages, look for the "Ads and Business Solutions" option and choose "Business Pages".

If you can't find the topic you are looking for, or if you can't find the answer you need, consider searching the topic on Google. Facebook's Help Section is fully indexed on public search, so it may be easier finding what you are looking for this way. (Feel free to send me an email at sueann@faceitsocialmedia.com and I will try to help as well!)

Another way to help answer a question you can't find in Help is to look for the option "Community Forum" (Figure 13). This forum allows Facebook Users from all over the world to ask and answer questions. When you choose one of the Community Help Topics, you will see a long list of questions that people have asked, along with any answers. Do any of these look like the same question that you have? Maybe their answer will help you. If you click on one of the Search topics above the list, then you will be given the option to ask your own question. Once you have participated in the forum by asking and answering questions, then you can check the status of these on the main "Community Forum" page.

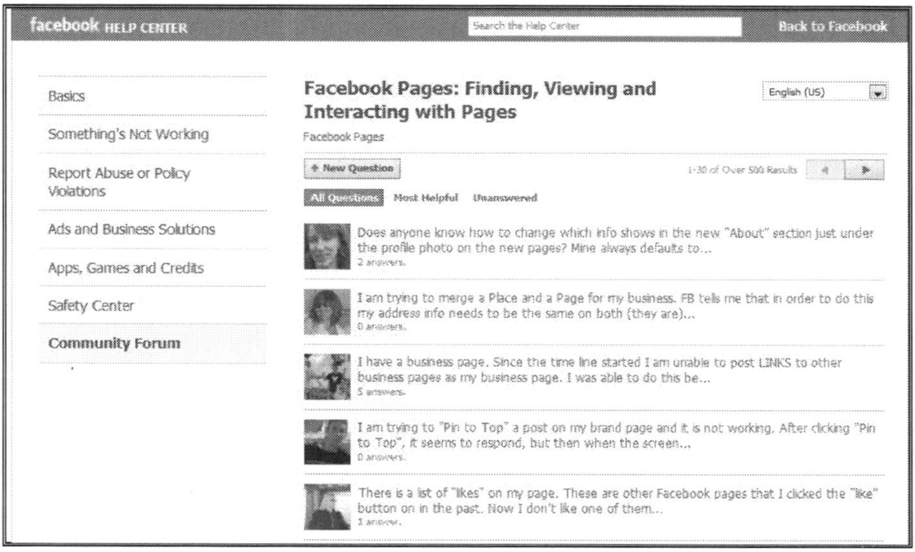

Figure 13: Community Forum

From the "Help" button on the Admin Panel, you can choose to take a tour of the new Page Timeline. The tour if very simplistic, but only takes a few minutes and may make you feel more comfortable navigating your Page.

The "Pages Product Guide" and "Learning Video" are links to a document and video that present basically the same information as the tour. Everyone has a different learning style, so one may be a better resource for you.

5.3   Cover Photo

The Cover Photo is an important feature of your Page. Because if the amount of room it takes up on your Wall, it is the first thing any Facebook User will see when they visit your Page. Use this image to set the tone for your Page. Use photos of your products, a menu item, artwork, or a photo of your business represented at a recent community event, or yourself at a speaking engagement. Try something a bit more abstract. You could even create of picture containing a collage of photos.

The Cover Photo should be at least 851 pixels wide x 315 pixels long for minimum resolution.

Facebook has very strict rules about what can and cannot be used for a Cover Photo. It is not meant to contain for a call to action, contact information, or other details that can be found in the "About" Section of the Page. In fact, try to limit the amount of text that you include in your Cover Photo.

To be sure that your Cover Photo conforms to Facebook rules, adhere to the following guidelines:

- Do not include special offers or purchase information
- Do not include contact information such as your email, phone number, address, or website.
- Do not refer to any Facebook features such as "Like our Page" or "Share with your Friend"
- Do not make any calls to action such as "Call today", "Download our app" or "Enter our contest".

5.4   Edit Page

On the Admin Panel, the first button, Manage, provides the option to "Edit Page". This option allows you to adjust your Page settings and set parameters as to how the Page will look to the world. It controls the "inner workings" of your Page, shows you what's "under the hood", how to get into the "back door", where the "magic happens", etc.

5.4.1   Manage Permissions

By default, when you select "Edit Page", the window that pops up is "Manage Permissions", which is actually the second choice on the list on the left-hand side of the screen (Figure 14). From this window, you can decide

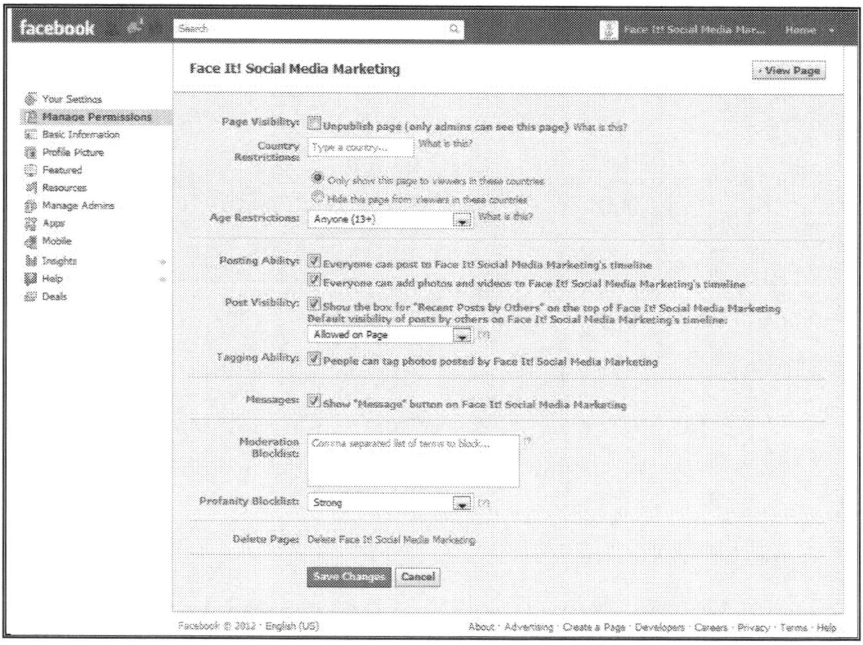

Figure 14: "Manage Permissions" Window

to "Unpublish page" which may be a valid option for you if you want to wait to make your Page public, both to Facebook search and public search engines, until after you have completely set it up and populated it with several posts, photos and links. Just remember to go back and unclick this option!

If you choose to have your Page published only in certain countries, you can specify that next in "Country Restrictions" option.

The "Age Restrictions" option allows you to limit those who can view your page to a specific age between 13 and 21 and over, or to specify that the Page is alcohol related.

The "Posting Ability" options lets you specify whether or not you want your Fan's posts, photos, and videos to show up on your Page's Timeline. Because social media is about sharing, only in rare circumstances will you not want your Fans' posts to be displayed. One example where my client and I decided to not allow Fans to post photos and videos was a children's dance studio. We did not want posts of the children and teens during their performances without permission from the studio director and parents.

The "Post Visibility" option allows you to include the box on your Page showing what other Fans have posted. Again, since the entire purpose of social media is interaction and dialog, which can only take place if your Fans are able to post on your Page and see what others have posted, you will want to check all three of these options.

If an inappropriate comment or post is made on your Page, you can delete the post, and even ban the user. Hover over the post, click on the blue "x" and choose "Delete". If you delete the post, you will also be given the option to ban the user completely.

Page Admins now have the ability to automatically hide posts which contain words which are specified, in addition to words and phrases commonly determined to be offensive. Note that the post will be shown in grey to the

Admins, but hidden completely from public view. The "Moderation Blocklist" allows you to enter specific words and thereby hide any posts that contain them. The "Profanity Blocklist" provides three options, "None", "Medium", and "Strong." Facebook has not publicly specified which words fit into the Medium versus Strong category, and only states that they are words generally agreed to be offensive but the "broader community."

The final option on the "Manage Permissions" page is "Delete Page." This gives you a way to stop and start over if you have determined that you used the wrong category. It is also the obvious choice if you need to delete your Page for whatever reason.

5.4.2   Your Settings

The first choice on the list on the left-hand side of the screen is "Your Settings." This window (Figure 15) allows you to choose how you want your posts displayed, and also whether or not you want your Page notifications to be sent to the email address of your Personal Profile.

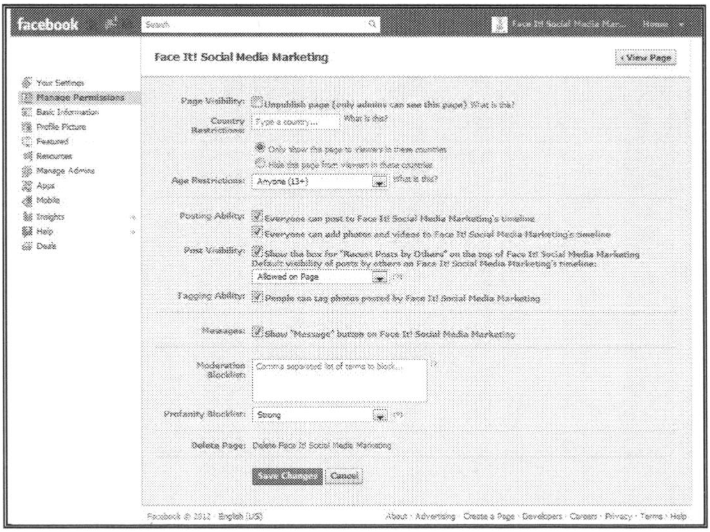

Figure 15: "Your Settings" Window

The "Posting Preferences" option lets you specify how you, as the Admin, want to have your posts shown. Do you want them to show as being posted by the Page or by your Personal Profile? If you check this box, then when you access the Page for which you are an Admin, then any post you make will have the Page's Profile Picture attached to it and the Fans will see this as a post from the Page. If you do not check this box, then any post that you make on that Page will have your Personal Profile's picture attached to it and the Fans will see this as a post from you personally.

Generally, as the Admin, you will want to have your posts come from the Page and will check this box. However, there may be times that you will want to make a personal comment on a Page that you administer. For instance, if there is an event or an interesting post that you, as an individual, not as the Page Admin, would like to comment on, you will want to comment as yourself. Did you attend a class, or have dinner, or read a posted link that you found intriguing? It wouldn't make sense for the Page to post a comment, but it would be beneficial for a post to come from your Personal Profile.

The option for "Email Notifications" allows you to decide whether or not you want notifications of new Posts or Comments sent to the email address you gave when you set up your Personal Profile. If you click on this option, you will receive an email to this address every time a Fan posts on the Page, Likes the Page, or Likes a post. This could get overwhelming as the Page matures and has frequent interactions with its Fans. But it is also helpful if you don't intend to be on Facebook daily and need the reminder to check on your Page.

5.4.3   Basic Information

The "Basic Information" form (Figure 16) is exactly that: where you put the basic information about your business. When a Fan is looking at your Page, they can access the "About" button below the Profile Picture.

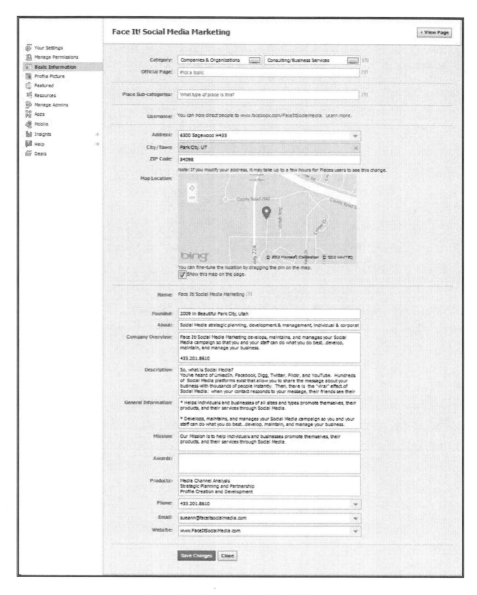

Figure 16: "Basic Information" Window

When you first created your Page, you specified a Page type and category. This will determine exactly what information is in the pre-formatted Basic Information template. Most fields are the same regardless of the Page type and category, but some categories allow different fields. For instance, a Restaurant/Cafe Page will have Food Styles, Payment Options and Parking availability, whereas a Movie will have a Release Date, and fields for listing principal.

From this window, you can create a Username, also called a Vanity URL, which is a custom URL unique to your Facebook Page. The Username will have the format "www.facebook.com/*username*", rather than a randomly generated URL with a long string of extraneous characters. This will allow you to have a much cleaner URL to share in your printed marketing materials. The Username must be unique, because it is a link to a specific page on the web, which just happens to be your Facebook Page.

Ideally, the username will be the name of your Page.

When you click on this option, you will be directed to use "Facebook as *Your Personal Profile*", it you aren't already. Then, a dropdown menu will appear listing all of the Pages for which you are an Admin. From here, you can type in the Username you'd like and see if it is available. Once you find a unique URL that you'd like to use for your Username, then you can select that. Note that, once you choose the Username, you cannot change it.

The "About" section in the Basic Information form is very important. This information will be shown in the on the left-hand side of the Page Wall, right below the Profile Picture, and right above the word About. When anyone visits your Page, the About field will be there for all to see (Figure 17). Take advantage of this premier location to tell people as quickly as possible about your business: who you are and what you do.

Note that you only have 255 characters in this section, so make it succinct and powerful! Choose every word and character carefully!

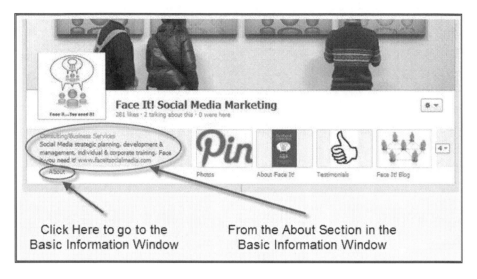

Figure 17: About

Think of About as an elevator pitch. It is a good idea to include your website and telephone number in this section so that people who come to your Page can see both immediately without having to click through a bunch of windows. Use About to make it easy for someone to see a quick summary of your business and find your contact information.

When someone visits your Page Wall, right below your Profile Picture and to the left of the Tabs, they will see the blue word About. Clicking on this will take them to the description of your Page taken from the Basic Information form. This one click will show that user everything they need to know about you in one quick snapshot.

When someone clicks on About, then they obviously want to know more, right? There have been so many times that I've searched Facebook for a company and then, when I found it and looked at their Basic Info screen,

I couldn't even tell where they were located! So give them as much information and make it easy. You need to go through the Basic Information field by field and fill it out completely. Include your address (a handy Google map will automatically be generated), hours of operation, and a detailed description and general information. Make sure you put your business email, phone number and website! Since Facebook Pages can be indexed by public search engines, be sure to include effective keywords in your Basic Information to help with search.

5.4.4 Profile Picture

This tab allows you to edit and change the Profile Picture for your Page. In this section, we will be discussing not only how to upload or change your Profile Picture, but also what type of image to use.

The Cover Photo and Profile Picture (Figure 18) are vital in setting the tone

Figure 18: Cover Photo and Profile Picture

for your Page. Since the Cover Photo takes up so much space, it obviously draws attention and creates an important first impression. However, users will only see the Cover Photo when they go to your Page. Refer to Section 5.3 to learn more about Cover Photos.

The Profile Picture, which is the square image shown on the lower left of your Cover Photo, is used to create the thumbnail, which is the image that "travels" with your Page. The Profile Picture is cropped to create the thumbnail, which is the image that is attached to your Page Name in search and to every post your Page and is seen by all of your Fans when they see your Post on their News Feed. Your thumbnail must help people immediately associate with your brand and differentiate your Page in Facebook search.

Since Facebook doesn't require unique Page names, there is a possibility that there are other Facebook Pages that have the same name as yours, so the thumbnail is the best way to distinguish your Page from others. When people search for your Page, the thumbnail image of your Profile Picture will show up with next to the Page name, so make sure the picture is something that will help them know that *this* is the Page they are looking for, something that helps them recognize your business and differentiate it from another with the same name.

When your Page's posts show up in your Fans' News Feed, your thumbnail appears just to the left of your post. When people are quickly scanning their News Feeds to learn about the latest and greatest from the Pages they Like, your thumbnail needs to draw their attention to your post. They need to recognize that this post is from your business, and since you *always* post interesting and compelling information, they will stop scanning their News Feed and respond to your post.

So what image should you use?

Your logo is an obvious choice. If your logo is prevalent throughout your branding, then people will see your logo on Facebook and recognize your business. But what if you don't have a logo, or you just don't want to use it? You have options limited only by your creativity. Some examples include your storefront with your signage, your signature product, your booth at an event, a coffee cup with your logo, or a staff photo (Figure 19).

Figure 19: Page Profile Pictures

What about your own picture? Unless you are a well known celebrity, I recommend against using a photo of yourself because it may confuse people. Are you posting from your Personal Profile or from your Page? If your Fans know your business but not you personally, they may wonder who this person is that is posting on their News Feed!

One of the Pages I Like in my Personal Profile changed their Profile Picture to include that of a model promoting their product. The Profile Picture was cropped so that the thumbnail showed this model's face, but nothing about the company. As I scrolled down my News Feed, I saw a post with a picture of a woman whom I've never seen before. Who is this person who hacked into my account? Even now that I know that this image is the Profile Picture for that Page, it still makes me pause when I see their post. Quite frankly, I resent that they may be trying to pose as a Friend rather than a Page, even though this is not the case at all.

If you must use your own picture as your Page's Profile Picture, then add something to the picture to differentiate it. Add the name of your business, a small logo in the corner, or your tag line.

In addition to the Edit Page option, you can also change your Profile Picture directly from your Wall with fewer keystrokes. Simply hover your curser over the small box to the left of your Page Name and at the bottom corner of the Cover Photo area. Click on "Edit Profile Picture" to show the menu of options. (You can also access this from the Admin Panel, Manage, Edit Page and then select the Profile Picture option.)

If you have already uploaded a photo that you want to use, then this image will be saved in your Facebook Photos library. You can use the first option "Choose from Photos" to help you find and select this image from your library for your Profile Picture. Or, you can choose "Take Photo" to shoot a picture with your webcam (but if you look anything like I do when you are working at your desk, this is NOT an option!)

To upload an image that is saved in your computer, choose the "Upload Photo" option. A search box will appear so that you can browse through your computer to find the image you want.

The image that you use for your Profile Picture must be at least 180 x 180 pixels to be accepted. However, the thumbnail that is linked to your Page on all of your posts and in Facebook search can only be 32 x 32 pixels, so choose your Profile Picture so that it scales neatly to create your desired thumbnail. Facebook will allow you to adjust and crop your Profile Picture into the square thumbnail format (or it will be done automatically).

You can adjust and crop your image with the simple tool Facebook provides by clicking on "Edit Thumbnail." You can access this by hovering over the Profile Picture box and choosing the last option (or by going into the Admin Panel as described earlier).

To edit the thumbnail, hover over the image in the box until you see the curser change to a crosshair (Figure 20). You can then click and drag the image around in the box to position it in the best spot.

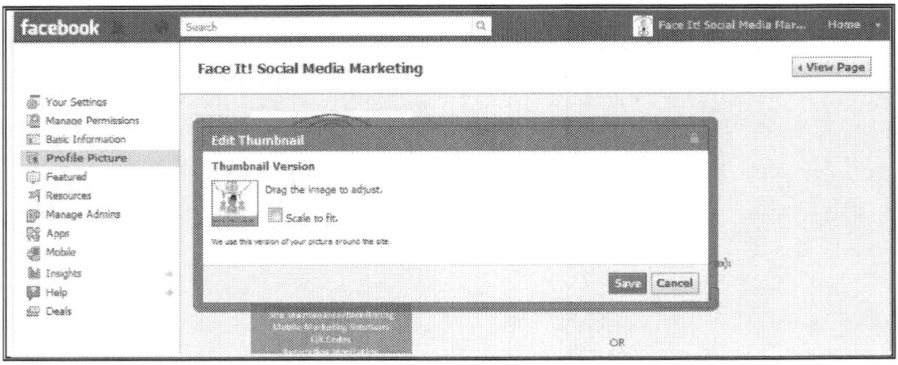

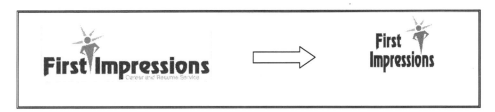

Figure 20: Editing Your Thumbnail

If you image is close to being shaped like a square, you can check the box called "Scale to Fit" and see how the image looks when automatically scaled to fit within the dimensions of the Profile Picture box.

It is very important to work with your Profile Picture fits properly in the thumbnail. Take the time to play with the image using photo editing software. If your logo is rectangular and you cannot fit it into a square thumbnail, then you may want to rethink what you want for your Profile Picture, or be creative! Figure 21 shows an example of a logo that was impossible to legibly fit within the constraints of the thumbnail dimensions, and how the logo was edited for Facebook.

Figure 21: Adjusting Your Logo to Fit in the Thumbnail

5.4.5   Featured

Your Page can also Like other Pages, just like individual Personal Profiles can Like Pages (Pages are not included in the number of Likes). This allows your Page to post on another Page's Wall and to also tag that Page. This increases your post's visibility because it may be seen by the other Page's Fans as well as your own.

The "Featured" window allows you to "feature" your choice of five of the Pages that your Page Likes (Figure 22). This is like putting their bumper sticker on your Wall.

Figure 22: "Featured" Window

In the "Featured" window, when you click on "Add Featured Likes", a pop-up box shows all of the other Pages that your Page Likes. Click on up to five Pages you want shown, or you can leave it to Facebook to randomly pick and display them.

The thumbnails for five of these Pages (either the five you choose or the five randomly picked by Facebook) will appear on the right hand side of your Page's Wall (Figure 23). When Fans view your Wall, they can see these thumbnails of other Pages that your Page is interested in and has Liked.

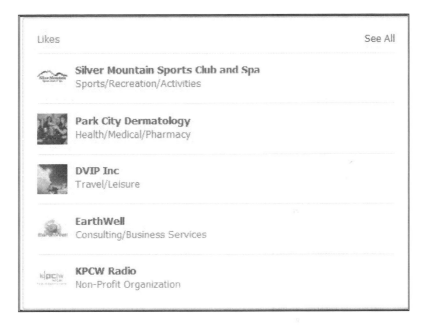

Figure 23: Featured Likes and Admins on Page Wall

If you are using "Facebook as Your *Personal Profile*", and you search for, find, and Like that Page, then your Personal Profile Likes the selected Page. The selected Page will not be a Featured Like of your Page and will not show up on the list on the left hand side of your Page Wall.

Earlier, when we discussed the difference between Facebook Groups and Pages in Section 3, you learned that the Admins for a Facebook Page are anonymous. This means that no one can see who the Admins for a Facebook Page are...unless the Admin chooses to show this by selecting the

"Add Featured Page Owners" option. If you click on this button, you can choose which, if any, Admins are shown to the Fans on the Page's Wall.

Generally, the Admins for a Page will remain anonymous. Many different Admins may be posting on the Page, or the Admins may change, depending on who is working for the business at any given time. However, if you are a small business, then in the eyes of your customer, you ARE the business, and it makes sense for people to see that you are the Admin. For example, a restaurant chain may have someone on staff acting as an Admin for the Page, in which case, they want them to stay anonymous. In contrast, a personal chef may want to show that they are the Admin of their own Page and, therefore, will choose this option.

5.4.6   Resources

Much of the content in this section can be found in Facebook's Help tool or other Facebook documentation. For instance, the option for "Best Practice Guide To Make Your Page Engaging" takes you to another Facebook administered Page where you can locate information and comments about this topic.

Clicking on "Advertise on Facebook" will allow you to create an advertising campaign for any of the Pages that you administer. (Note that you must be using "Facebook as *Your Personal Profile*" and not as your Page in order to create an ad.) Facebook ads are a very effective and lucrative way to promote your business. Facebook has done a great job creating a simple interface for creating and targeting pay-per-click and pay-per-impression ads.

You can choose between creating your ad from scratch, using the copy from a previously run ad, or creating an ad based on the activity of your Fans. A "Sponsored Story" is an ad created with a Fan's Profile Picture stating that this Fan Likes the Page, or one that shows a Fan commenting or Liking a particular Post, chosen randomly by Facebook. See Section 9.0 for a complete description of how to create a Facebook Ad.

The "Select a username" option allows you to generate a custom URL, also called a Vanity URL, which is unique to your Facebook Page. This is the same tool as we discussed in Section 5.4.3. The Username will have the format "www.facebook.com/*username*", rather than a randomly generated URL with a long string of extraneous characters. This will allow you to have a much cleaner URL to share in your printed marketing materials. The URL must be unique, because it is a link to a specific page on the web. Ideally, the Username will be the name of your Page.

Remember that Page names are not necessarily unique, so you may have to be creative when choosing your Username.

When you click on this option, you will be directed to use "Facebook as *Your Personal Profile*", if you aren't already. Then, a dropdown menu will appear listing all of the Pages for which you are an Admin. From here, choose the applicable Page and type in the username you'd like and see if it is available. Once you find a unique username that you'd like to use for your Vanity URL, then you can select that. Once you choose the URL, you cannot change it.

The "Tell Your Fans" option is the same as the "Import Contacts" option that was discussed in Section 5.2.3. You will be asked to link to your gmail, Yahoo, or other web-based email server or an email client via a .csv (comma separated value) file. If the email for your contact is the same for which an individual has linked to their Personal Profile, then they will see the suggestion for the Page the same way that your Friends would. If not, then they will receive an email inviting them to join Facebook.

The "Use Social Plug-ins" option allows you to generate the necessary HTML code to link your Facebook Page to your website. You can choose between any number of options, including a simple Like, Send, Subscribe, or Comments Button, to more interactive plug-ins like Activity Feeds, Recommendations, Like Box, and Activity Feeds. These social plug-ins are important to add to your website or blog.

You may be asked for your Facebook ID when you try to generate the HTML code for a plug-in. To find your ID, you will need to go to your Page's photos. It won't matter if you are using "Facebook as *Page Name*" or "Facebook as your *"Personal Profile*." When you go to the Photos, click on any photo and look at the browser window (Figure 24). There will be an

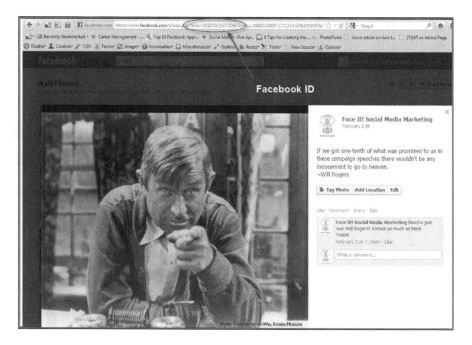

Figure 24: Facebook ID

address listed with a string of numbers attached. Look the string of digits after the characters "?fbid=" is your Page ID. You will notice that this set of numbers will remain the same while the first set of numbers will change as you look at different photos.

The "Link your Page to Twitter" does exactly that. This is a hand tool that allows all of your Facebook Page posts to be automatically tweeted on your

Twitter feed. To create this link, make sure you are logged into your Twitter account. Then allow the app access and simply follow the directions.

The "Additional Resources" section contains links to Facebook User Groups and Help Center. It never hurts to take time out and read these, as Facebook is frequently changing mechanisms on their site unannounced. However, unless you plan to become a Facebook app developer, you can ignore this.

5.4.7 Manage Admins

Through the "Manage Admins" option, you can view everyone who is an Admin for the Page, and add or delete Admins. To add a new Admin through this option, the person must already be a Fan of the Page, and you must know the email that the person used to set up their Facebook account. If you are using "Facebook as *Your Personal Profile*", you can type in one of your Friend's names and make them an Admin.

There is another way to access and manage your Admins. When you are using Facebook as a Page, look at the blue bar at the top of the Page. When you click on the Likes icon on the upper left hand side, a pop-up box will appear and you will see the Profile Picture of everyone who Likes the Page (Figure 25). On the right-hand side, you will see the "Make Admin" button. Clicking on that button will make that person an Admin. They will receive a notification that they have been made an Admin of this Page.

If the button says "Remove Admin", then that person is already an Admin. Click on this button will to remove this person as an Admin of the Page. This method is a bit more cumbersome if you have dozens or hundreds of people who Like the Page, because the list is not in alphabetical order, rather, the list is populated by the most recent new Like at the top down to the first Like at the bottom.

Figure 25: "Manage Admins" Window

5.4.8 Apps

There are thousands of Facebook applications that will make your Page more interesting and engaging for your Fans. When you create your Facebook Page, it is already loaded with a few default Applications: Photos, Videos, Events, and Notes. As you load new apps, they will populate this list also and can be accessed from this window.

The applications that you install can be seen on your Page's Wall. The four boxes on the right under the Cover Photo are always visible (Figure 26). However, you can have as many as twelve application boxes that can be accessed by your Fans.

Figure 26: Applications Displayed On Your Page

The Photos application is always the first application and cannot be moved. The remaining eleven (or as many as you are using) can be organized so that you can choose which other three are always visible. Simply click on the number with the down arrow to the right of the fourth box, then hover over the box that you want to move, click and specify which other box you want to switch places (Figure 27).

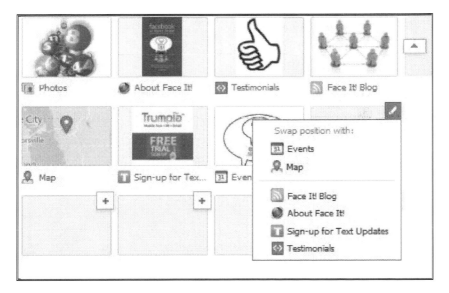

Figure 27: Swapping Application Positions on your Page

When you are in Applications Window of Edit Page, you will see the list of applications that are installed on your Page. Below the description of the app are options such as "Go to App", "Edit Settings", and "Link to this Tab."

Choosing "Go To App" should take you to the application on your Facebook Page for apps such as Photos, Events, Links or Notes. However, the link is not consistent if you are using "Facebook as *Page Name*" compared to using "Facebook as *Your Personal Profile*". Likewise, the link is not consistent between the different applications. If you have downloaded a 3rd party app, then Go to App will take you to that application for editing. However, if you are using Facebook as a Page and select "Go to App" for a 3rd party app, then you will be directed to switch to using "Facebook as *Your Personal Profile*".

When you are adding applications, realize that many are very powerful, helpful and useful, while others are less reliable and robust. Before downloading an app, make sure you review it carefully and trust the developer.

The "Edit Settings" option allows you to remove the application's tab from the left hand side of your Wall. This option may also have additional tabs depending on the app.

Clicking on the "Link to this Tab" option will provide you with the unique URL for that tab on your Facebook Page. For instance, if you want to be able to link your website to your Facebook Events, then you can use this URL to link.

5.4.9 Mobile

In today's mobile society, over 80% of the new cell phones sold are smart phones. Some want this just to be able to have mobile internet access, while others want to be connected 24/7 via their smart phone. The "Mobile" window allows you to set up your mobile phone to access your Facebook Page when you are not at your desktop or laptop computer.

You can send an update to your Page via mobile email, through a text message from your phone, or by downloading a Facebook app to your phone. The "With Mobile Web" option provides another link to generate a Vanity URL.

5.4.10 Insights

Insights are a wonderful tool that Facebook has developed to help you determine the effectiveness of your Page. Until you get 25 or so Fans, your Page will not generate Insights, as there is so little data to present you're your Page is first created. Once the number of Likes grows, your Insights will help you determine at a glance which days garner the most interactions, what time of day is the most effective, and what posts receive the most responses. Insights will also show you the gender, age and geographic demographics of your Likes. Section 8 discusses Insights in depth.

5.4.11 Help

Click here for Help. Need I say more? Well, actually, yes. I'm not thoroughly impressed with Facebook's Help Center. When I have a question on a Facebook mechanism, I've often found that it is more helpful to search for it on Google.

We talked about the Help Center in Section 4.4.5. The Community Forum allows you to ask other users for help. From any of the options, you will see a list of topics, followed by a list of related questions asked by Facebook Users from around the world.   Feel free to peruse these questions and answer some if you want.   To ask your own question, click on the appropriate topic and then click on the "Ask Question" button. You will be sent an email to your Personal Profile's email address if anyone submits an answer to your question.

If you do, however, have a question for Facebook and you cannot find the answer, follow these steps to contact their Help Desk. First, from the Facebook Help Center main page, choose "Something's Not Working."

From there, choose the appropriate topic from the "Report A Broken Feature" list. Look for the "My bug is not listed above" and click on that. You will see "Please submit but reports only here". Click on the word "here" and you will be prompted to explain the problem or question you are having. A screen shot of the page with the problem will help clarify your question. Once you have submitted your problem or question, Facebook will send you an automated response stating that they have received the message and, depending on how busy they are, may or may not be able to respond. It is always worth a try!

5.5   The Blue Bar

No, this is not a cool night spot where Facebook employees go after work. The blue bar on top of the Facebook window provides shortcuts to a few tools. However, the most important thing to remember about the blue bar is that it refers the entity that is in control of your Facebook session: either your Personal Profile or your Page.

When you are using "Facebook as *Your Personal Profile*", the right hand side of the blue bar will show the name and the thumbnail for your Personal Profile. In this case clicking on your name will take you to your Personal Wall, and clicking on the Home button will take you to your Personal News Feed.

When you click on the Friends/Fans icon, the one that looks like two silhouettes, you will see any new Friend requests (Figure 28). Clicking on the icon that looks like a conversation bubble will show you any messages that you have received from Friends, and the icon that looks like the world will show you any notifications for your Personal Profile.

Figure 28: Friends/Fans Icon Using "Facebook as *Your Personal Profile*"

When you are using "Facebook as *Page Name*", the blue bar will refer to your Page instead of your Personal Profile (Figure 29). The right hand side of the blue bar will show the name and the thumbnail for your Page, and clicking on the Page name will take you to your Page Wall, while clicking on the Home button will take you to your Page's News Feed.

Clicking on the Friends/Fans icon will now show you the list of your Page's Fans. But there are a few other things you can access from this icon as well.

When you click on the icon, a list of a few Fans will appear, with "See All" button below. Click on this and you will see a larger list with a scroll bar, as well as the buttons to "Make Admin" or "Remove Admin". Next to that button is a blue X that will allow you to delete or block a Fan.

On the top of that list, you will see a drop down menu allowing you to view "People", "Pages", "Admins", and "Banned". If you choose "Pages", the list of Pages that Like your Page will be shown. The blue X will let you delete

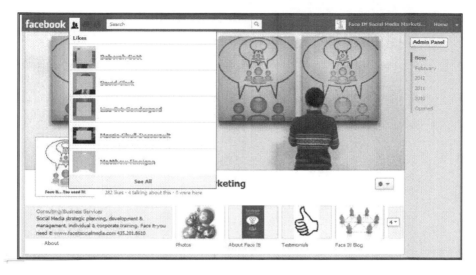

Figure 29: Friends/Fans Icon Using "Facebook as *Page Name*"

them if necessary. Choosing "Admins" will show you a list of Admins for the Page with the option to remove them.

Choosing "Banned" will show you a list of any Pages or Fans that you have banned from your Page. You can "Unban" them from this window.

Clicking on the conversation bubble icon will show you any messages that you have received from Fans, and the world icon will show you any notifications for your Page.

5.6   Home/News Feed

The News Feed is found by clicking on the Home button on the right hand side of the blue bar (Figure 30) when using "Facebook as *Page Name*". It is a running list of the posts made by those Pages that your Page Likes. Consider it your Page's own personal Facebook Newspaper, only you get to

Figure 30: Your Page News Feed

choose the news source that is shown. The posts made by your Page are not shown on the News Feed.

The News Feed is only seen by the Admins. When someone comes to your Page they cannot see your News Feed. They can only see your Wall.

The only way to view your Page's News Feed is to use "Facebook as *Page Name*." When using "Facebook as *Page Name*", clicking on Home on the right side of the blue bar will take you to the News Feed. If you are using "Facebook as *Your Personal Profile*," then clicking on Home will take you to the News Feed for your Personal Profile.

On the left side of the News Feed screen, you will see the thumbnail for your Page rather than the larger image that you see when you are looking at the Wall. You can click on the thumbnail or the name of the Page to be taken to the Wall. Below that, you will see the options "News Feed", "Insights", "Events", and a list of applications loaded on the Page.

When you hover over "News Feed", you will see a pencil on the left side. Click on this and you can choose "Edit Settings" options such as which Page's posts to hide. Note that if you scroll to the very bottom of your News Fee, "Edit Options" will do the same.

Clicking on any of the other options on the left side will take you to that tool or application.

Notice that you can create a post from the News Feed just as you can from the Wall, including adding photos, links, videos, and questions.

The grey line above the News Feed and below the Composer contains the word "SORT" on the right side followed by a down arrow. Clicking this will allow you to view posts by Top Stories or by Most Recent. Top Stories are those with the highest EdgeRank (Section 7.1), while Most Recent are in reverse chronological order.

The right hand side of your News Feed provides you an Insights Summary, including the number of Likes, how many are Talking About This, and the Weekly Total Reach. You can click on the blue See All to be taken to the Insights for your Page (see Section 8).

5.7   Accessing Your Page

When you log onto Facebook, you are automatically taken to the Wall on your Personal Profile. From here, there are several ways to access your Page. The way you access your Page will determine whether you are using "Facebook as *Page Name*" or "Facebook as *Your Personal Profile*".

Begin typing the name of your Page in the Facebook search box. A dropdown menu will appear and you will find your Page on the list (Figure 31). You will be using "Facebook as *Your Personal Profile*." The Pages that you Admin will automatically show up at the top of the list.

Figure 31: Accessing Your Page From The Search Box

Another way to access your Page is from the down arrow the right hand side of the blue bar (Figure 32). When you click and hold on the arrow, you will see a list of all of the Pages that you administer, with a scroll bar is necessary. Click on the Page and you will be taken to taken to that Page using "Facebook as *Page Name*."

You can also access your Page from your Personal News Feed. When you see a post from the Page, you can click on either the Page's thumbnail or the name of the Page and you will be taken to the Page using "Facebook as Your *Personal Profile*."

Figure 32: Accessing Your Page From The Blue Bar

Another way to access your Page is from the left hand side of your Personal News Feed screen, under your Profile Picture (Figure 33). Look for the list of the Pages that you administer. Click on the Page and you will be taken to the Page using "Facebook as *Your Personal Profile*."

Figure 33: Accessing Your Page From Your Personal News Feed

Once you are in the Page, if you are not already using "Facebook as *Page Name*", you will see on the right hand side the option to use "Facebook as *Page Name.*" Likewise, if you are on the Page and already using "Facebook as *Page Name*", you will see on the right hand side the option to use "Facebook as *Your Personal Profile*".

6.0   Posting on Your Page

What is on your mind? What do you want to share with your Fans? The Composer (Figure 34) is the tool you use to type in the message, or status update, and upload the photo, link, video or question that you want to deliver to your Fans. It is arguably the most important mechanism of your Facebook Page.

Figure 34: The Composer

How to post your message is one thing, *what* to post is something entirely different. What will you post to create engagement on your Page? To encourage dialog? To get more Fans?

First, we will discuss how to create posts. We will discuss what to post in Section 7, including tips on posting compelling content and a discussion on EdgeRank, Facebook's algorithm for determine which posts get posted on the News Feeds of your Fans.

6.1   Status

Status updates are the most basic way to communicate with your Fans. These types of updates are text only, with no video, photo, or link attached.

While there are many times when posting simply words when you share is satisfactory, make an effort to include a photo, video, link or question in your message. This will make your message much more interesting and attention grabbing, as well as taking up more eye-catching space on your Page's and Fans' Walls.

6.2   Adding Photos and Videos

Photos and videos can help make your post more interesting and more attention grabbing on your Fans' News Feeds. Don't have a photo? Then go to Google or Yahoo! and search on images that pertain to your message. When you find one that is attention grabbing and appropriate, then save it to your computer. Just be sure that the image isn't copyrighted!

When you have a photo to include in your message, you can type your message first in the Composer text box and then click on "Photo" to upload, or click on "Photo" first and then add your message (Figure 35). You will be give three options: "Upload a Photo from your drive", "Take a Photo with your webcam", or "Create Photo Album".

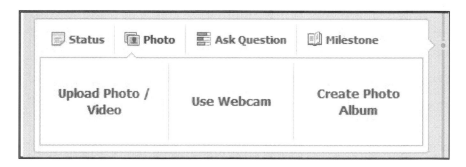

Figure 35: Adding Photos and Videos

If you click on "Upload a Photo", you will be shown the "Browse…" button. Clicking on this button will direct you to your computer file system, where you can then navigate through your computer to find the picture that you want to upload. When you choose the photo that you want to upload, the file location for that photo will be loaded and ready to share.

If you choose the section option, "Take a Photo with your webcam", then make sure you are out of your pajamas and your hair is combed.

The option to "Create Photo Album" is a good choice if you have many photos from an event or multiple photos of a product. When you click on this option, you will be directed to your computer file system and allowed to load any number of photos. Once uploaded, you can create a name for the album, specify where the group of photos were taken, and also give a brief description of each of the pictures. You can also choose which photo you want for the album cover. When you click "Post Photos", then the creation of the new album will appear as a status update.

Every time you add a photo, your Photo album gets updated. The first tab shown on your Page Wall will be a link to your Photo albums. You can also access if from your News Feed. Additional pictures can be added to albums after the album has been created and published.

What about video? Video is king! It has quickly become the medium of choice for sharing information. Video blogs, video tutorials, music videos, informational videos, laughing babies, and mischievous cats. We can watch and listen to the video while we multitask. We can get the information we want without having to stop and READ! Whatever the reason, the world loves video.

This Composer allows you to add videos that you have either already stored on your computer or create via your webcam at the time you are posting. If you are recording your video on your webcam, be sure to have the latest Adobe Flash Player installed.

A complete list of video file types is given in the Facebook Help section, but MP4 seems to work the best.

If you want to show a video that is on another website, such as YouTube or Vimeo, you are actually adding a link instead of a video. It just so happens that, the URL that you are linking to contains a video.

If you make a mistake and post the wrong photo or video, don't worry! If you have not yet completed the post, just click on the Status option and you can start over. If you have completed the post, you can always delete it by hovering over the post until you see the down arrow appear on the right hand side. Click on that and choose "Delete Post."

6.3   Adding Links

Often, you will find a link to an article that you want to share with your Fans. This may be something that you have written on your blog, or an interesting or funny piece that you found elsewhere. This is a great way to share important and valuable information with your Fans and help make your Page more interesting.

When you want to share a Link with your Fans, you need to include the URL in the text of the message you are sharing in your post. Type your comment in the Composer and then type or paste the URL that you want to share. When you hit the return key after typing in the URL, you will be able to see how the link will appear in your post.

The way the site that you've linked to is coded will determine how it appears in your post, and this is totally unrelated to Facebook. Usually, the title of the article that you have selected will appear, along with the first few lines of the body of the article, and any number of thumbnails from which you can choose the image you want to show up in your post. However, sometimes only the name of the main landing page from that site appears. Sometimes no thumbnails will be attached. If either of these happens, go ahead and click on Share and see what the post looks like. You can always delete the post and try again. Test the link to make sure that it is going to the article that you want.

If more than one thumbnail appears, you can cycle through them and pick the one you want. If you don't like any of the thumbnail options, you can choose "No Thumbnail." If no thumbnail is attached (again, this is totally dependent on how the site is programmed and is unrelated to Facebook), or you don't like any of the thumbnail options, yet you still want to add an image then choose "No thumbnail", and add your own photo instead.

6.4   Asking Questions

Questions and polls are fun ways to engage your Fans and to get their opinions. It is easy for your Fans to click on an answer without having to type in a response. Easy is good.

Start by typing in a simple question in the "Ask something…" text box. Next, click on the blue "Add Poll Options" and create a list of possible answers. You can enter as many poll options as you want. When you start typing, a drop down menu of Pages will appear in case you want to link to these. Just ignore these drop down choices and keep typing in the option you want to add. At the bottom, you have the option to allow others to add their own choices.

When people respond, their vote is tallied next to the option they chose (Figure 36). You can click on the results and see exactly who voted for what option. This is a great way to see what your Fans enjoy and how they feel about certain topics.

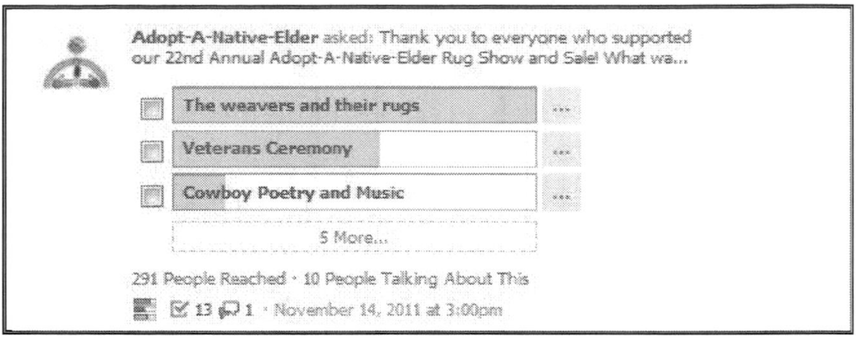

Figure 36: Fans Love Questions!

6.5   Milestones

Milestones (Figure 37) are an interesting way to share information about important dates and past events in your business. Using the Composer to create a Milestone allows you to draw special attention to an event or special occasion. You can create a Milestone to announce when you moved into your new location, when you reached your 500th Facebook Fan, when your company received a prestigious award, or when you have an open house or key event.

Figure 37: Milestone

6.6   Events

Facebook Events (Figure 38) are a great way to get the word out about a special promotion, occasion, or happening. "Events" is an application that is preloaded onto your Page when you create it, regardless of the type or category.

Figure 38: Facebook Event

To access Events initially, you must go into Edit Page and then click on Apps. From the list of applications, choose Go To App under the Events listing. This will take you to the tool that will allow you to create your event. Once you have created an event, then the Event tab will be displayed in the boxes below the Cover Photo.

The Events app is pretty self-explanatory. Fill out the Event Name and the time. You have the option of adding an end time of you desire. For the location, be sure to put the street address, as the application will like to a handy map for your guests to refer to for directions.

Next, type in the details of the event. You have unlimited characters available to you so be as descriptive as you can. Unfortunately, you cannot add a link in the details. To add a link, you must post it on the event wall after the event is created.

What about the following privacy settings? Do you want to make this event public so that everyone can see? Do you want your guests to be able to invite other guests? If the event is Public, then everyone will be able to see the event information, including event posts, photos and videos, and will be able to share it with their Friends. The event will also be found in Facebook and internet search results.

If the event is not public, then you, as the Admin for the Page, can decide who to invite. Only those who have been invited can see the details of the event. You can decide if guests can invite friends.

On the left hand side, you will find the button for adding an event photo. Be creative! Don't use the photo that you use for your Page's Profile Picture.

When the event is created, a Wall is also created that is unique to that event so that people who are invited can communicate and post information or comments. If you have a link to the event that you want to share, this is where you will share it, rather than in the event description.

Once your event is over, it will be archived. When you are using "Facebook as *Page Name*", go to your Wall and click on the Events tab below the Cover Photo, you will see button to create an event along with a list of past events.
If you are using "Facebook as *Page Name*" and are on your News Feed, then click on the Events tab on the left hand side. You will see the message "You

don't have any events", a Create Event button, and also a drop down menu with a magnifying glass and down arrow. Clicking on this will allow you to see upcoming and past events.

Facebook also allows you to export your events to your Apple iCal, Microsoft Outlook, and Google Calendar. Pretty handy.

6.7   Pinning a Post

Sometimes a post is important enough that you don't want it to get lost in the Timeline, but you don't want to repost it every day or so. In this situation, you can Pin a post to the top of your Wall so that it stays in that position even if you make subsequent posts later (Figure 39).

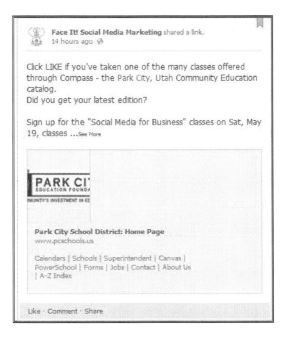

Figure 39: Pinned Post

Pinning a post does not change the width of the post on your Page Wall. However, it does add a small orange flag to the top right corner of the post and keeps that post on the top of the Wall to draw attention. Note that a post can only be pinned for seven days. After the seventh day, the post will revert back to its place in the Timeline on the Wall.

Only one post can be pinned at a time. Also, pinning has no effect on the post in your Fans' News Feed.

Hover over the post and look for the pencil button that will appear. Clicking on the pencil will allow you several options, one of which is Pin to the Top. Once the post is pinned, you can hover over the post, click the pencil again, and then the post will revert back to its position in the Timeline on the Wall.

6.8   Highlight a Post

When you post something using the Composer, you can also give some extra attention to the message. Highlighting a post causes it to span the entire width of your Page Wall, making it stand out more when a Facebook user visits your Page (Figure 40). Highlighting has no effect on the post in your Fans' News Feed the way pinning does.

Hover over the post and look for the star icon that will appear. Clicking on the star will highlight the post. Once the post is highlighted, you can hover over the post, click the star again, and then the post will switch from the highlights format and revert back to the regular size.

6.9   Changing a Post

When you hover over a post that you have created on your Page, you will see the pencil icon. Clicking on the pencil will allow you to change the date

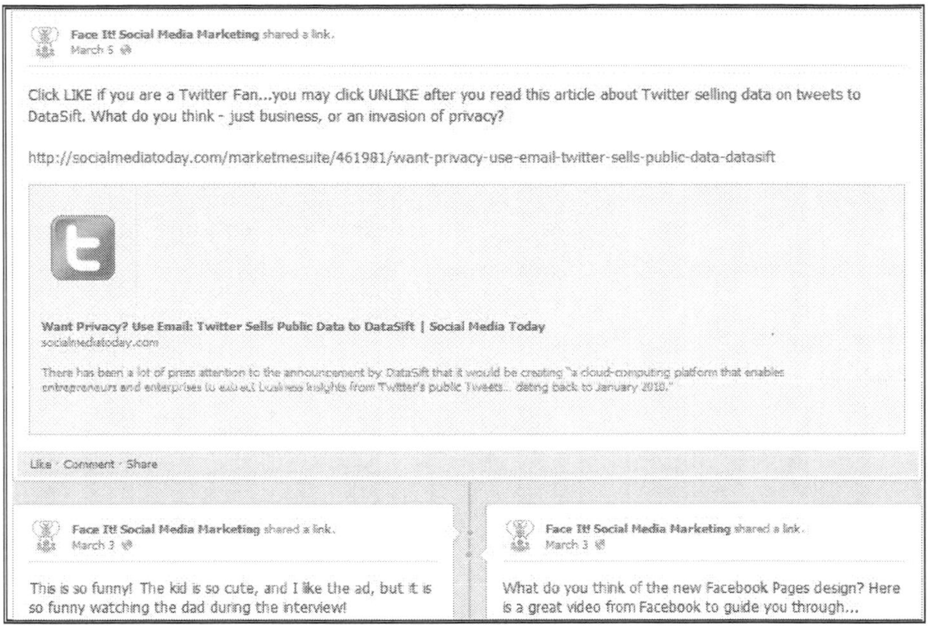

Figure 40: Highlighted Post

of the post, which is helpful if you are posting about an event in the past, but want the post to look like you entered it at that time.

You can also choose to add a location. If your post is location specific, for example, a community event, speaking engagement, or open house, it adds interest to the post to include the location.

You can also hide a less interesting post from your Page, as well as reporting and marking as spam any inappropriate posts from Fans.

6.10   Deleting a Post

A misspelled word, a typo, incorrect grammar, wrong photo or video...no matter how many times I proofread something, it never fails that I'll find an error! Isn't that frustrating?

Unfortunately, with a Facebook post, you cannot go back and correct an error. Just like an email, you can't hit "unsend". Your only option is to delete the post and start again. This isn't so bad if you catch the post immediately. But if you find the post hours or days later, you know that someone has seen the error. If someone has shared the post with their friends, then it is out there in the wild world of the web and those posts can't be deleted.

If you realize that you have uploaded the wrong photo, link or video, or don't like the question you posed *before* you hit the Share button, simply click on Status and you can start over without losing the text that you have already written, and without having to post the update and then delete it.

To delete the post that has already been shared, simply hover over your post and you will see the blue world icon with a down arrow. Click on that and you will see the option to Delete Post.

If you have linked your Facebook Page to your Twitter Profile or other social media site so that you automatically post your updates, then your update with the error is on your Twitter feed as well. You will need to go into your Twitter profile, find the post, and delete it. Again, if it has been retweeted or replied to by others, those can't be deleted.

7.0   Engaging Your Fans

So now you *how* to post to your Facebook Page, but *what* should you post? What will help you get more Fans and more engage the Fans you already have?

We talked about the basic principles of social media in Section 1.1. Remember that people must give you permission to share your information with them. When a Facebook User Likes your Page, they have given your business permission to share on their News Feed.

What will entice someone give you permission? Your job is to create posts that make their lives easier, more fulfilled, more interesting, healthier, ...better. How does your Page benefit them in their personal lives or in their business? People want to be informed and entertained. They want tips, secrets, special offers, and access to deals and information. They want your Page to add value to their lives!

Remember, also, that "word of mouth" is the best advertising you can't buy. Your content needs to have information that people will want to share with their Facebook Friends. When they share with their Friends, their Friends will see that the Post originated from your Page and will be more likely to check out the source of this great information.

Today, people do not want to be "sold to". I heard somewhere that "If you talked to people the way advertising talked to people, they'd punch you in the face."

Yes, the end goal is to sell our products or services and make money. But with social media, it is more about creating the relationships and brand advocates. If you have a good and reliable product or service, and you have earned the respect and enthusiasm of your clients, their support will do the selling for you.

Don't make every post about selling. Think about at 4-1 ratio: post four value added posts for every sales related post. Go ahead and create posts about your weekly or monthly specials, about your products' features, or about the benefits of your services, but don't let those be the only things you posts. Post information that is helpful, unique, entertaining and that adds value. Something that makes your Fan think, "Wow! I didn't know that! That was really helpful. I can't wait to tell my Friends!" Or "That was really funny! I can't wait to tell my Friends!"

And remember the golden rule: Never post anything you wouldn't want your grandmother to see. Be courteous, thoughtful, and professional with a human twist. Mind your manners and watch your spelling.

Before we get into specific posting tips, it is important for you to understand EdgeRank and how it affects how your posts are published in your Fans' News Feeds.

7.1 EdgeRank

EdgeRank is an algorithm used by Facebook which assigns a value to a post by a Page or Profile, and the uses that value to assume the importance of that post to the Fans or Friends to which the user is connected. EdgeRank is similar to the search algorithms you may be aware of with Google, Yahoo, MSN, and other public search engines.

Facebook tries to determine, based on the user's behavior on the site, what posts they will find the most interesting and useful. The algorithm uses this information to calculate an EdgeRank score for the posts, and then populates a user's News Feeds according to each post's score. While Facebook has made the high level attributes of this algorithm public, the details are highly confidential, so this discussion must prefaced with the statement that there are factors that we are not privy to that will affect EdgeRank.

Facebook calls every interaction that a user makes an "Edge." A status update, profile update, attaching a link or photo or video, Liking a Page, comments on someone else's post, etc. are all called Edges. Since EdgeRank determines what goes onto any user's "Top News" option of the News Feed, that unique News Feed for each user is basically a list of Edges customized for that user based on their Facebook behavior. The "Most Recent" option of the News Feed is just that – a collection of the most recent posts by Friends and Pages without regards to EdgeRank.

EdgeRank uses three factors in its algorithm: Edge Weight, Affinity, and Time-Decay (Figure 41).

$$\sum_{edges\ e} u_e w_e d_e$$

u_e - affinity score between viewing user and edge creator

w_e - weight for this edge type (create, comment, like, tag, etc.)

d_e - time decay factor based on how long ago the edge was created

Figure 41: EdgeRank Algorithm

Edge Weight assumes the importance of a post. For instance, photos, links, videos, and polls cause a higher Edge Weight than a simple post with no attachments. For this reason, having an attachment to your posts will increase the likelihood of the post appearing in your Fans' or Friends' Top News Feed. So not only does adding something to your post make it more colorful and take up more space on the screen, it will give your post a higher Edge Rank.

Affinity is basically a rating of how often a Facebook User communicates with or views a Friend's or Page's activity. It is basically a rating of how "friendly" that User is with that Friend or Page. Even if the User doesn't write on their Wall or comment or share their posts, just visiting their Page or Profile can increase their Affinity.

However, it is important to remember that this is one-way. When you visit a Page or Profile, their posts will probably begin appearing more often in your News Feed, because you have increased *your* Affinity with *them*. However it does not mean that your posts will appear in their News Feed. *They* have to visit and communicate on your Page or Profile in order to increase *their* Affinity with *you*.

You cannot control another User's Affinity with your Profile or Page. All you can do is control your Affinity with their Profile or Page. Do what you can by posting engaging information to encourage their interaction with you, which will help improve their Affinity with you.

Time-decay is related to how recently the post was published. As the time since the post increases, the decay also increases, and the importance probably decreases. If someone hasn't been on Facebook in several days, when they do log in, they will see posts that are very recent, rather than posts that are nearly a week old. They will have to dig to find those posts they missed while they were not active. Time-decay is a more obvious and objective component of Edge Weight, because if the post is old, it is probably not that terribly relevant and the news may be stale.

It is important to understand that an EdgeRank is assigned to each Post created by a Page or Profile. However, the value for that Post is different for each Fan or Friend (or Page) to which that Page or Profile is connected. So a Post made by Joe's Pizza Page will have a different EdgeRank for Amy's Personal Profile than it will have for Mary's Personal Profile or even for John's Pizza Delivery Page. And vice versa. Joe's Pizza Page will have a different EdgeRank for Lisa's Personal Profile than Lisa's Personal Profile will have for Joe's Pizza Page.

EdgeRank can be valuable, since it weeds out potentially unwanted information from your News Feed. If you think about, it, without EdgeRank, every post from every Fan with whom you are connected, along with every post from every Page that you Like will show up in your Personal News Feed. It would take forever to read and sort through what is important and what is not! One of my Friends Likes nearly 2000 Pages and is Friends with over 1500 other Facebook Users. Can you imagine his News Feed without EdgeRank?

EdgeRank can also be frustrating because a computer algorithm may not really know what we find interesting and useful! For instance, you have Liked a Page or Friended someone because you are interested in what they have to share. You may or may not interact with their posts, but you still want to see those posts. They may share something that you will find very important, but because you haven't interacted with their Page or Profile, the EdgeRank for that post may not be very high. You may not be given the opportunity to see those posts on your Top News Feed. To ensure that you do, you must play the game and comment on their posts, share their content and write on their Wall to let Facebook Know that you are interested in that Friend or Page.

With regards to a Page, it is important to understand these three factors of EdgeRank to increase the odds of appearing on your Fans' Top News Feeds. So how can you improve your EdgeRank? It may seem obvious, but let's discuss it anyway.

First of all, it is important to try to encourage your Fans to increase their Affinity with your Page. How do you do this? Start by asking questions in your posts. Use the questions to prompt a response or reaction. When a Fan does respond, respond back and begin a discussion. Have you tried Polls? This is a great way to get Fans involved. This will increase your

Affinity with that Fan, and hopefully, others will jump into the fray, increasing your Affinity with them as well. Tell your Fans to "Click Like" if they agree with what you have posted. Don't be afraid to ask your Fans to share your posts with their Friends.

Second, make sure your posts are interesting and encourage interaction and dialogue. Always include a photo, video, or link attachment in each and every post. Whether you add a photo or image that enhances or describes your message, or you are commenting on an interesting link or video, this will help improve your EdgeRank. Furthermore, when you add one of these elements to your post, the post itself will take up more room on the News Feed, making it easier for the post to stand out from other, less interesting posts.

Third, post regularly so that you always have content that is fresh. You may not want to post every day, but do post several times a week. Also, know that it is helpful to be aware of when your audience is using Facebook so your posts will be timely. If your target market is folks who work the graveyard shift, then chances are they will be sleeping in the morning, and any posts that you make early in the day may not be seen simply because they aren't logged in. Check your Insights to determine when you get the most response from posts.

Another important thing to glean from this information on EdgeRank is that the number of Likes is no indication of your Page's success. Just because someone Likes your Page does not mean your posts will show up in their Top News Feed. Yet people can still look at and interact with your Page even if they have not Liked your Page. So, don't let a small number of Fans for your Page discourage you. Most local brands have only a few hundred Fans. By the same token, don't let the number of Fans you have give you a false sense of security. A thousand Fans means very little, other than bragging rights, if those Fans don't interact with your Page.

7.2 Tips for Posting Compelling Content

How are you going to connect with your customers and prospective clients? How will you get the word out about your company's great products and services? What is *compelling* content?

The discussion about EdgeRank should have convinced you that every single post you make should have a photo, link, video, or question attached.

Every. Single. One.

Let's discuss other things you can do to help engage your Fans and entice new ones.

7.2.1 How Often Should You Post? When?

You can ask 10 different people and you will get 10 different answers. When someone Likes your Page, they have allowed your Posts to be added to their News Feed. They have given your Page their permission. This person may like 10 Pages or 100 Pages. You want your Page's posts to show up in their News Feed, but nothing is more annoying than to see a stream of posts from the same Page.

My suggestion (and again, I know you want it) is to do no more than one or two posts a day, and post 3-5 times a week. This gets your message out without monopolizing the News Feeds of your Fans. Posting less than once a week implies that you may not be fully participating and interested in Facebook. Infrequent posting will affect your EdgeRank and, when someone does come to your Page, they will wonder why you aren't participating. Are you still in business? Do you care? People expect to find your business on Facebook and they expect you to be posting regularly.

Review your posts and see which ones are getting the most activity. Are you able to determine a pattern? Do you see more comments and likes in the morning or evening? On Mondays or Saturdays? Every business is different, and it is up to you to determine the habits of your Fans. If you get the most interactions on Sunday afternoons, then that is when you should be posting. By all means, post at other times as well, but it is worth the effort to determine if there is a most effective time of day and day of the week.

7.2.2   Share Relevant, Useful and Timely Information

Did you just read an interesting article about a community issue or something that affects your industry? Did you hear a good joke? Share it! There is so much information out on the internet that your Fans will appreciate you weeding through the mess and being their source for articles worthy of note.

If you have an amazing insight or have found a great article or video to share, don't just share the juicy information, share what you think about it. Then, ask a question of your Fans. Tell them to click Like if they agree.

Make sure the content is fresh and new. Why bother your Fans with posting an article that is 6 months old and irrelevant or out of date? I get frustrated when I see a post with an article or video that sounds interesting. Then when I open it and find it is from over a year ago and the information is not current (and often incorrect because it is outdated), I can thank that Page for wasting my time. I will think twice before I click on another link that they post.

Remember: your job as the admin is to provide information that makes your Fans' lives *better*. Remember clipping services a few years back? These people provided a great service by scanning newspapers and magazines and literally clipping out articles that they thought would interest their client. Consider your Page a clipping service, or better, a personal secretary who reads the mail, email, and newspapers, and only forwards on the important stuff. Your Fans will begin to look to your Page for the information that is of interest to them and grateful that you've done the legwork and saved them time and energy.

7.2.3   Tagging and Posting on Other Pages

We have discussed how Pages can Like other Pages. One of the advantages of Liking Pages is that your Page can post on that Page's Wall for all of *their* Fans to see. Wow! Now your post may have just been seen by all of *their* Fans with your Page's thumbnail right there on the Wall for all to see! Think about how many more Facebook Users you can reach! Oh – the visibility! (If the Page does not allow others to post on their Wall, then you are out of luck. But it's worth a try.)

When you post on another Page, it does not show up on *your* Page's Wall. However, when you Tag a Page, then the post will show up on *both* your Wall and the Page's Wall (if they allow it and if the EdgeRank is high enough).

To Tag a Page, create your Status Update so that it includes the name of the Page in the text. When you type in the text, use the "@" symbol before you start typing in the Page name. As you start typing in the name, you will see a drop down box with Pages that begin with the same letters. When you find the Page that you are wanting to Tag, then select that from the drop down menu.

I know this sounds frustrating, but sometimes this does not work. Sometimes the Page does not allow others to write on their Wall. Sometimes it's just a bug in Facebook. It seems to be a delicate feature and not as robust as it should be. If it doesn't work, then go ahead and post the update on your Page, then copy it and try to post it directly on the other Page. It will have the same effect but will take two steps. But you should definitely try to Tag other Pages as often as possible, as it increases your visibility. When it works, it is a beautiful thing.

When you are using "Facebook as *Page Name*", and you search for and Like a Page, then your *Page* Likes the Page. Your Page can then post on that Page's Wall and Tag that Page. However, if you are using "Facebook as *Your Personal Profile*", and you search for and Like a Page, then your *Personal Profile* Likes the Page. Your Page can then post on that Page's Wall and Tag that Page. The Page (or Pages) that you Admin may or may not Like the same Pages that your Personal Profile Likes. So, it is important to pay attention to which is in control of your Facebook session so you know which Pages you can post to or Tag.

7.2.4   Create Fan Interaction

Social media is all about conversation and creating relationships. You want your posts to be engaging and to invite dialogue. It is great if your post is seen by your Fans, but what is even better is if your Fans start talking about your posts. Or better yet, start a conversation amongst each other about your posts. Your job is to encourage this conversation and give it a little push in the right direction.

Remember that our world is all about speed and sound bites. Don't be verbose in your message. Be succinct and straight to the point.

When creating your posts, don't be afraid to ask your Fans to click Like. "Click Like if you're going to our Open House tonight!" "Click Like if you are a baseball fan!" When your Fans comment on or Like a post, acknowledge this. Respond to their comment, even if it is a simple "thank you". Ask an additional question.

Ask questions. Don't just share a link or video: ask your Fans what they think. Make the question simple, as many people will ignore the question if the answer will be long and drawn out. Try something like, "Share 3 words about what you thought about today's class." Or, "What was your favorite Super Bowl commercial?"

They can always post more if they want, but ask a question that allows them to answer quickly with as few words as possible. People are always in a hurry and will be more likely to respond if the requested response is short.

Are two or more Fans talking about your Post? Join in the conversation and encourage the dialogue! When you see that your Page has a new Fan, welcome them with a "Thanks for Liking our Page" message on your Wall. This is the "social" part of "social media".

Encourage your Fans to share your Page. Just ask! "This is a great article! Share it with your Friends!" "We're at 497 Fans! Share our Page with your Friends and let's hit 500 today!"

Have you found certain Fans are more active than others? Then chances are, they are more active on Facebook in general. Make a special effort to engage them, as this will help your posts be seen by their Friends when they share and respond. Consider interviewing them for your Page!

What if you get a negative post? This may be this is an opportunity to turn a negative into a positive. Respond to the negative comment or complaint and do what you can to resolve it! Often, an unhappy customer who has their problem solved quickly and easily turns into a brand advocate. If others see this process and realize that your company really cares about its customers and makes the extra effort to address and fix problems rather than ignoring them, then you have just won them over as well.

If you do find a post on your page that is inappropriate or spam, then consider deleting the post and evening banning that Fan from your Page.

7.2.5   Like, Comment and Share

Another simple and effective way to engage your Fans and create interaction is to participate in the conversation of other Facebook Users and Pages.

When you notice a post on your Page's Wall, either in response to one of your posts or to a post by a Fan or a Page that Likes your Page, don't ignore it. Respond! Click Like if someone made an interesting statement on one of your posts. Even better, post a comment. The comment you post will come from the Page with the Page's Profile Picture attached. (Note that, if the button in your Settings option of Edit Page is not checked, as discussed earlier in Section 4.4.2, then the comment will come from your Personal Profile, with your Personal Profile's picture attached.)

Sharing posts is another easy way to communicate with other Facebook Users. When you are using "Facebook as *Page Name*", then Sharing allows you to post the same story on your Page's Wall. When you are using "Facebook as Your *Personal Profile*", you will share the story on the Wall on your Personal Profile. Think about this. If you have posted something on your Page, then go back to your Page and share it so that it shows up on your Personal Profile's Wall for all of your Facebook Friends to see – and share with their Friends.

When you are using "Facebook as *Page Name*", and you are in your Page's News Feed, look for interesting and relevant posts by the other Pages that your Page Likes. Like their posts or make comments about them. Your Likes and comments will show up on that Page's Wall, for all of their Fans to see!

7.2.6   Coordinate Your Marketing Strategies

Facebook isn't a stand-alone marketing tool. Are you using email? A website or blog? Direct mail? Other social media sites? It is important that your branding is consistent throughout the tools that you are using.

Share new content from your blog on your Facebook Page. Link your Facebook Page to Twitter and LinkedIn so that your updates are posted on all three sites.

You can use other automated tools to share on other sites as well, but these LinkedIn and Twitter have very robust applications that make sharing with

Facebook simple and painless. Just remember that, when you use an automated tool, such as Hootsuite or Tweetdeck, the status update will specify the name of that tool. The formatting may also be compromised. It loses the personal touch of posting "by hand".

Use the social plug-ins that you can create in the Resources window of Edit Page and put badges on your blog and website so that it is easy to share your message and Like your Page.

Create a link your Facebook on your email signature.

Add the custom URL or even just the Facebook logo to your business card, brochure, advertisement, and any other written marketing material.

Let the world know your Page is on Facebook!

7.2.7   Keep Business and Pleasure Separate

As mentioned before, Facebook Personal Profiles are entities designed for you to interact with friends and family. This is the mechanism you will use to share videos of your son's winning touchdown at the high school football game, your birthday celebration, or of the big fish you caught on vacation (photo shopped, of course).

Your Facebook Page is where you interact with business associates, customers, prospective clients, and anyone who shares an interest in your area of expertise or product. Do you want them to see your family pictures? Do you really want your customers to know that you spent two weeks in Bali? Yes, some of these are also friends and family, but many are not. *Who* do you want to see *what*?

There will be those who argue, and the call is totally up to you. I recommend keeping the two separate. Often, I will post something on my Page and then share it on my Personal Profile, but rarely do I post personal information on my Page.

7.2.8   Contests and Sweepstakes

People love to get things for free! People love to play games and win prizes! And what better way to promote your Page and your business than to hold a contest or give away a free gift?

A Contest is any type of competition that requires some specific talent or skill and is judged.   A Sweepstakes is a random selection of a winner. Facebook does not consider coupons or rebates to be either of these types of promotions.

Before you jump in and launch a contest or sweepstakes you need to be familiar with Facebook's rules and terms for running such a promotion. Facebook has strict guidelines for running a contest or sweepstakes.

As far as the Facebook rules go, the main idea is that you cannot use Facebook mechanisms to run the promotion and that you must not imply Facebook's endorsement.   If Facebook finds that you are running a promotion and not adhering to their guidelines, they could shut down your entire Page.   Be sure to check Facebook's promotional guidelines at https://www.facebook.com/promotions_guidelines.php when you are considering running a contest or sweepstakes.

In a nutshell, these are the basic rules that you must abide by:

- You cannot make Liking the Page the entry to the promo, although you can restrict the promo to people who Like the Page.
- You cannot make people Tag or mention the Page as a requirement to participate
- You cannot require people to write on the Wall
- You cannot use the Like Button or Questions to have people vote for the winner
- You cannot ask people to upload a photo or video to participate
- You must run the promo through an app.

- You cannot notify the winner via Facebook but you can announce the winners on your Page (we will use a sign up page and collect emails)
- You must indemnify Facebook and specify that the promo is not endorsed by Facebook and that Facebook is not collecting information from participants.

Facebook requires that you use a Facebook Application to administer the promotion. There are many applications that you can load onto your Page. If you see applications on other Pages, there will generally be a badge along the bottom or side giving credit to the application developer, so you can search for that application. Many developers charge for their applications, but there are also several good and easy to use free app, such as like FreePromos, WildFire, and Fanappz. Do a public search for free Facebook applications and see what you can find that fits your needs.

7.2.9   Other Posting Tips

This isn't really about posting, but it is a good way to keep your Page fresh: update your Profile Picture. I like to change my Page's Profile Picture every month or two. The "weebles" in my logo will wear a winter scarf, party hat, hold an American flag, or something relevant to the season. Or I'll put up a QR Code or a photo of me at a speaking engagement or workshop. Create just enough of a change that when your Fans see a post with a new thumbnail, it will grab their attention.

Does your Page have several Admins? Consider having the Admins sign their posts so that the Fans know which posts come from which Admins. It breaks through the corporate barrier and reminds your Fans that there are real people who are doing the posting. This helps create a sense of community and relationship.

8.0   Insights

Facebook has done a superb job creating a free tool for measuring the engagement and effectiveness of your Page. This is possible because Facebook retrieves an immense amount of data on its nearly 1 Billion users. You may not like this from a user's perspective, but from a business owner's take, you will appreciate all of this information and how it can help you improve your interaction with your Fans.

Your first visit to Insights can be overwhelming. Let's start slowly.

You can access Insights from your Wall by clicking on the Admin Panel button. From there, click on Edit Page and choose Insights.

Note that only Page Admins can access Insights for a Page. Also, Insights are only generated for Pages once they receive 30 or more Fans. The details on all of the Insights windows are substantial, which makes legible screen shots difficult.

8.1   User Activity

This first line of information on the main Insights Window (Figure 42) provides important data to determine how large your fan base is and how they are engaging with the content that you are sharing. "Total Likes" tells you the number of Fans of the Page, and the following number, "Friends of Fans" tells you the number of 2nd degree connections with whom you have the opportunity to connect if all of your Fans interact with your Page. Next to these numbers is a percentage that tells you the growth or decline in these numbers.

The "People Talking About This" and the "Weekly Total Reach" tells you how many of your Fans have interacted with the Page and how many News

Figure 42: Page Insights: User Activity and Page Post Table

Feeds your message has appeared on within the past week. These are graphed weekly.

The "People Talking About This" number is visible to the public when they visit your Page. Think about our inherent "mob mentality" and strive to create posts which cause people to comment, tag, like, and share. If Facebook Users see a large number of others "talking about this", then they may be interested in see what all of the fuss is about.

The Overview Graph shows purple dots, the size of which represents the number of posts you made on a given day. When you hover over these dots, you can see the number of posts, the number of people that post reached, and the number of people talking about that post.

8.2   Page Posts Table

The "Page Posts" table lets you determine the efficacy of each post in terms of reach and engagement. Using the drop down menu, you can select from different types of posts to see how engagement varies from photos to video to links, etc.

You are able to click through and see the post completely, including the time of day. Don't underestimate the importance of the timing of your posts! Do you get more interactions when you post on a weekend morning or weekday evening? This isn't to say that you should always post at the same time on the same day, but it is helpful for you to understand your target audience.

You can see the effectiveness of each post in terms of the "Reach", "Engaged Users", "Talking About This", and "Virality".

"Reach" tells you how many unique people have seen this post on their News Feed. EdgeRank is what will determine the reach. Interesting and timely posts will reach more people. Fans with a high affinity will see your Page's posts more frequently.

"Engaged Users" are the number of people who have clicked on your post for any reason: to like, comment, or share, or click through a link. These people are showing that they are interested in your post by clicking on *something*.

"Talking About This" is a subset of this number and tells you how many people liked, shared or commented on post.

The "Virality" measurement gives you an idea of the possibility of your Fans sharing your Post. This percentage is simply the "Talking About This" divided by the "Reach". So, if 25 people are talking about a post that reached 2000 unique people, then the virality is 1.25%.

Look at the posts that have done well and determine what has caused the great performance. When you have determined what works best and what doesn't you can recreate your success in subsequent posts.

8.3   Likes

The second option under Insights is "Likes". This window provides detailed information about the demographics of the people who Like your Page (Figure 43). In addition to gender and age, you can see where in the world these Fans come from, literally. In addition to this information, the chart below lets you know how many new Likes (and Unlikes) you have received daily, and where these Likes have come from.

8.4   Reach

The Reach window (Figure 44) lets you know the demographics of the people your Posts have reached during the time period specified. This is interesting because you can determine how certain post performed across age groups, or with men versus women.

How did you reach these people? Were your paid advertisements more effective than your organic efforts (posts simply appearing in News Feeds)?

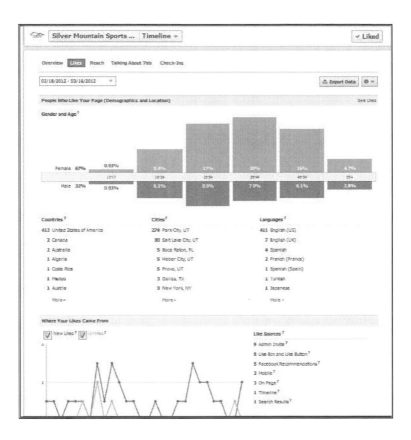

Figure 43: Page Insights - Likes Window

The "Unique Users by Frequency" tells you how many times people viewed your content. How many viewed your posts once? How many viewed it 10 times? 20 times? Remember EdgeRank? Those who viewed your content multiple time have developed a higher affinity with your Page than others. You need to know who these influencers are and how to continue to engage them and encourage them to share.

The next graph shows you how many times your Page was visited, and how many of these visits were by new people, rather than current Fans.

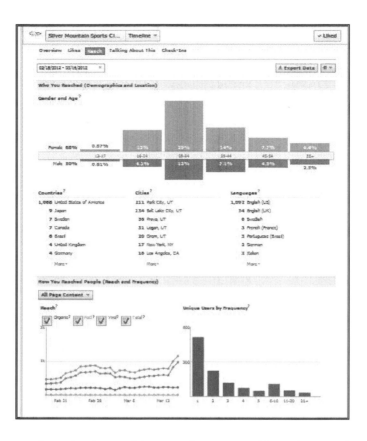

Figure 44: Page Insights – Reach: Demographics and Users

Scroll down the page to see the "Visits to Your Page" graph and following two tables (Figure 45). These show you which of your Page's tabs were viewed by visitors, and from what external websites (other than Facebook) new visitors came to your Page. This last bit of information is important, because it tells you if people are coming to your Facebook Page from your website, blog, another social media site like Twitter or LinkedIn, or some other location on the web. Facebook allows you to communicate with people in ways these other sites cannot. This metric helps you determine how effective you are in driving traffic to your Page.

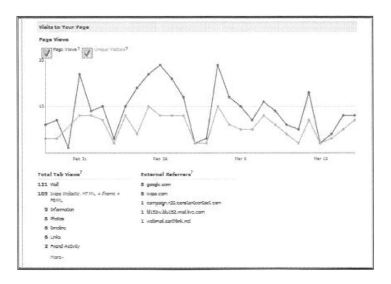

Figure 45: Page Insights – Reach: Visits

8.5   Talking About This

The graph on the "Talking About This" window (Figure 46) shows demographic information about the fans who are creating stories, through comments, likes, etc, about your Page. This data is only available if more than 30 people have been talking about your Page in the date range selected at the top of the graph. The "How People Are Talking About Your Page" tells you the type of posts that are inviting the most interaction, and hence, virality.

8.6   Check-Ins

Check-Ins data is relevant for businesses that are also Places where Fans can check in, such as a store, club, or restaurant (Figure 47). This metric indicates the demographics about those who have checked-in and whether they used the Facebook site or a mobile device.

Figure 46: Insights - Reach: Talking About This

8.7   Export Data

The information from Insights can be exported to an Excel file (.xls) or a text file (.csv) for analysis, if you so desire.

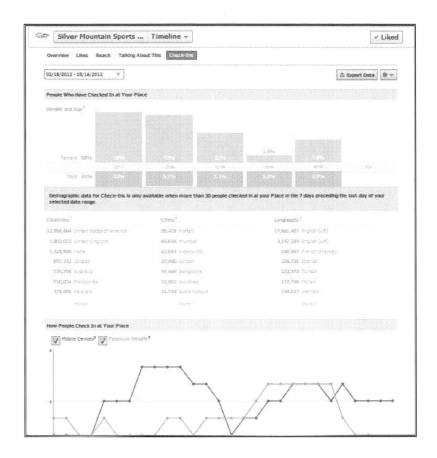

Figure 47: Insights - Check-ins

8.8 Weekly Facebook Pages Update

Although this is not a section found on Insights, the Weekly Facebook Pages Update email (Figure 48) is another great engagement tracking tool provided to Page Admins.

Every Admin of a Page will receive a weekly (or somewhat weekly) email that reports basic interactions with the Page. If you are the Admin of more

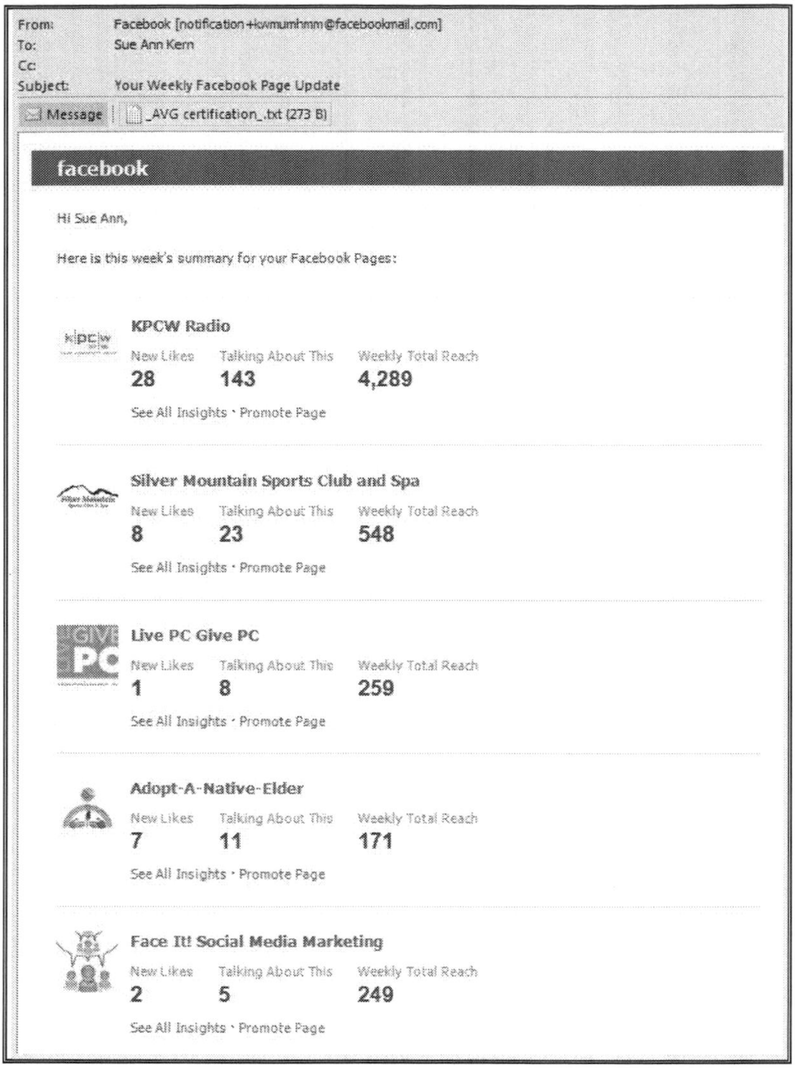

From: Facebook [notification+kwmumhmm@facebookmail.com]
To: Sue Ann Kern
Cc:
Subject: Your Weekly Facebook Page Update

Message   _AVG certification_.txt (273 B)

facebook

Hi Sue Ann,

Here is this week's summary for your Facebook Pages:

KPCW Radio

New Likes   Talking About This   Weekly Total Reach
28   143   4,289

See All Insights · Promote Page

Silver Mountain Sports Club and Spa

New Likes   Talking About This   Weekly Total Reach
8   23   548

See All Insights · Promote Page

Live PC Give PC

New Likes   Talking About This   Weekly Total Reach
1   8   259

See All Insights · Promote Page

Adopt-A-Native-Elder

New Likes   Talking About This   Weekly Total Reach
7   11   171

See All Insights · Promote Page

Face It! Social Media Marketing

New Likes   Talking About This   Weekly Total Reach
2   5   249

See All Insights · Promote Page

Figure 48: Weekly Facebook Page Update Email

than one Page, then only one email will be sent to you which will contain information on all of the Pages.

This email gives you a brief synopsis of how your Page(s) performed the previous week. In addition to seeing the total number of Likes, you can view how viral your messages have been by reviewing the "Talking About This" number and the Weekly Total Reach. You want to see an increase in these numbers (percentage in green) rather than a decrease (percentage in red). Look back on the week and see what you did right and wrong.

From this email, you can hyperlink back to each Page and the Insights for that Page. Seeing too much red? Then click on "Promote Page" and you will be magically taken to the tool to let you create a Facebook Ad.

8.9   What To Do With All This Data?

Yes, all of this is information overload. What do you really need to look at and what can you ignore? Unless you are a statistics nut and get your kicks reviewing mountains of data, you really only need to pay attention to a few topics.

First of all, determine your target audience. Women in their 40 - 50s? Anyone in their 20 - 30s? What areas? Are you creating posts that attract the attention of my target audience?

Secondly, pay attention to the Page Posts Table. This gives you loads of information to determine which types of posts are creating the most buzz. Look at what posts are creating the most interactions. What was posted? What was interesting? What time of day? What posts were not successful? Study this information and recreate the recipe.

9.0   Facebook Ads

Facebook Ads have proven to be a very effective way to draw attention to your Page, to get new Fans, and to promote a special event, product, or offer. If it wasn't effective, it wouldn't be so profitable: in 2011, Facebook made $3.2 billion in advertising revenue, up nearly 69% from 2010!

Facebook Ads are not just for large Pages with thousands of Fans. They can be just as effective for a small Page with a local following. Remember, the average user spends a little over 15 minutes a day on Facebook, more than any other internet site. When a Facebook User sees your ad impression on the right hand side of their Page, they may or may not click through to your Page, but they will be affected by the marketing concept known as the "nudge effect".

The "nudge effect" can best be explained with this analogy. When a user sees your ad on their Facebook Wall, they may or may not be interested in your product or service *at that exact moment*. They may not click through. However, the user can't help but make a mental note (consciously or sub-consciously) of the ad and your brand for future reference. The more frequently the user is exposed to your brand, the more likely the user will remember the brand when the time comes that they are interested in your product or service.

With Facebook Ads, you can choose to pay for the ad each time it is displayed (impressions), or only when a user clicks on the ad. Pay-for-Impressions (CPM = Cost Per 1000 Impressions) costs less per unit, however, Pay-per-Click (CPC) is more cost effective because you only pay when the user makes the action of clicking through.

Facebook also lets you set a daily budget, as small ($1 minimum) or as large as you like. The budget can also be set for the "lifetime" of the ad, rather than daily. You can easily target the ads for geographic area, gender, age and interests, as well as set a timeframe for running the ad. When the ad is running, you can make changes, extend the schedule, or even delete the ad.

There are many ways to locate the tool to create an ad for your Page,

- Click on the blue "Advertising" option on the right hand side line at the very bottom of the screen.
- Go to "Edit Page" and click on "Advertise on Facebook"
- Click on "Promote with an Ad" on the right hand side of the Page Wall
- From Insights, click on "Promote your Page"

To create your ad, you must be using "Facebook as *Your Personal Profile*". This is because Facebook will be asking for payment information that will be linked to your Personal Profile.

9.1   Design Your Ad

The first step in creating and designing your ad is the basic design and wordsmithing (Figure 49). If you manage multiple Pages, you will be able to access and create an ad for any of the Pages.

If you have already created an ad for a Page and simply want to duplicate or modify that existing ad, you can click on "Select Existing Creative" and choose the ad you want to use.

You can specify the destination of the ad to be an external URL, such as a special landing page on your website, rather than your Facebook Page. But one of the reasons you are running a Facebook ad is to gain more Fans and visibility for your Page. I suggest having the user land on your Facebook Page and then they can be directed to your website after they have clicked Like.

Figure 49: Facebook Ad Design

There are two types of ad: "Sponsored Stories" and "Facebook Ads".

"Sponsored Stories" are ads randomly created from Fan interaction on your Page. These include when someone Likes your Page, when the check-in to your place, or when someone Likes a post on the Page.

A "Sponsored Story" features a Friend of the Facebook User who sees the ad. A user will see that their Facebook Friend has Liked a Page, or has checked-in, or has Liked a post.   This is utilizing the word-of-mouth marketing concept: if your Friend Likes something, then chances are, you will too. These ads use the Profile Picture for the Page along with the Profile Picture for the user's Friend featured in the ad.

 "Facebook Ads" are ads that you create with your own image and verbiage. A "Page Post Ad" allows you to choose a particular post to use for your ad, using the thumbnail for the Page. A "Facebook Ads for Pages" allows you to enter the verbiage and image of your choice. You can choose which tab on your Page that you would like the user to land on when they click through.

Generally, you will want the user land on your Page Wall, unless you have a custom landing tab with a special offer. However, be creative and think outside the box! If you have a special photo album that you've loaded with photos of a product or event that you are promoting, consider having the users land on that instead.

The title, 25 characters, will always be the name of the Page, unless you are directing the user to an external URL. Note that, for Pages with long names, the title will be truncated to 25 characters.

The body of the ad can contain up to 135 characters. Be succinct and creative, but avoid excessive capitalization and exclamation points. Facebook may deny your ad for these. Use keywords to help with search and help viewers relate to and respond to the ad.

Find an image that is catchy, not necessarily your logo or Profile Picture. The maximum image size is 110 pixels wide x 80 pixels long. Since the image will be small in the impressions, make sure it is clear, simple, and not too busy.

Notice that you will be able to see the preview of the ad and make changes as desired before the ad is published.

9.2   Targeting

Facebook allows targeting to help you direct your ads to the people who may be the most interested (Figure 50). You don't need to pay for ads being directed to people who are not your target audience, or places where you do not even conduct business. Notice the "Estimated Reach" box on the right side. This displays your targeting options and tells you how each of these options affect the number of Facebook Users your ad can reach, and hence, the potential cost of your ad.

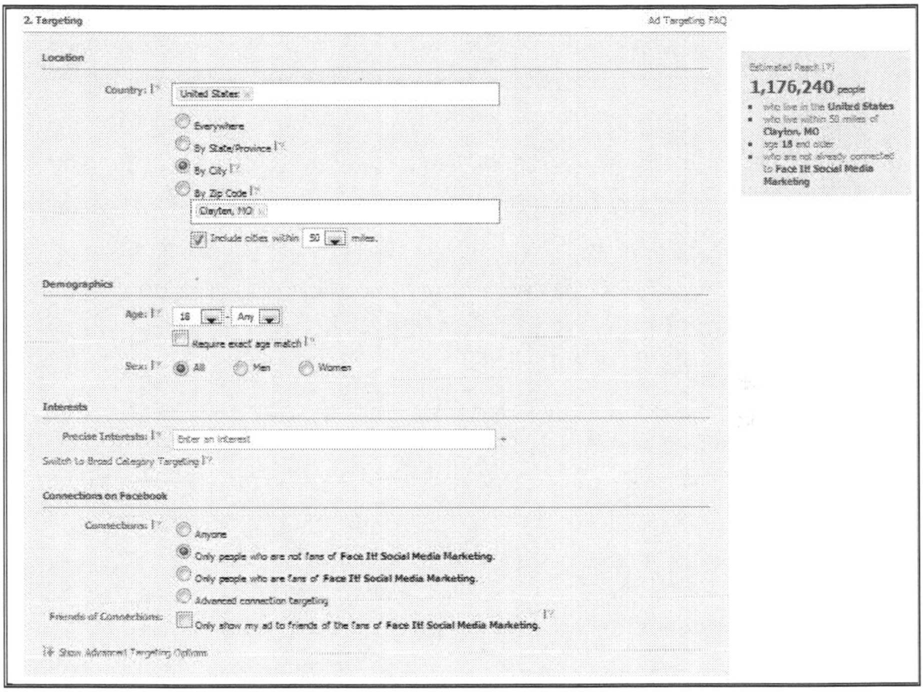

Figure 50: Facebook Ad Targeting

Geographic targeting allows you to narrow down the location by country, state, or to within 10, 25 or 50 miles of a particular city or even zip code. Gender and age targeting allows you to specify your audience even further.

The "Interests" section allows even more specific targeting. You want to target individuals who have listed "baseball", or "Italy" as an interest in their Personal Profile. As you start typing, a drop down menu will appear allowing you to click on the interest of your choice. However, I suggest ignoring this targeting option. Why? Once you select an interest, only people who have listed this specific and particular interest will be included in your targeting. What about the other Facebook Users who like Italy, but didn't put it in their profile? You have excluded all of these users from your targeting. Look what happens to the "Estimated Reach" when you choose an interest. You can delete the interest by clicking on the X in the box next to the name of the interest.

The next targeting option, "Connections on Facebook", allow you to specify which Facebook Users you want to see impressions of your ad. Anyone means users who already Like your Page along with others who don't (yet). If your goal is to attract new Fans, then you may not want to choose this option, as it may cost you to needlessly have impressions on the Walls of those who already Like your Page. For this purpose, you can choose "Only people who are not fans of *Page Name*".

If you are running a special for your Fans that is not meant for the general Facebook public, choose the "Only people who are fans of *Page Name*" option.

The "Advanced Targeting" option allows you to target Fans of other Pages that you administer. If you are managing two Pages that may hold similar interests for users, you can target the ad for one Page towards the existing Fans of another Page. Or vice versa, by specifying Pages whose Fans you don't want to target. Finally, you can target the ad only to Friends of the Fans of the Page.

Advanced Targeting also allows you to specify relationship status, language preferences, education and workplaces listed by Facebook Users.

9.3   Campaigns, Pricing, and Scheduling

Next we get to the real meat of the subject: how much will this cost?

The Campaigns, Pricing, and Scheduling section (Figure 51) allows you to create a name for your campaign for future reference. This will help you find the ad if you want to run it again down the road.

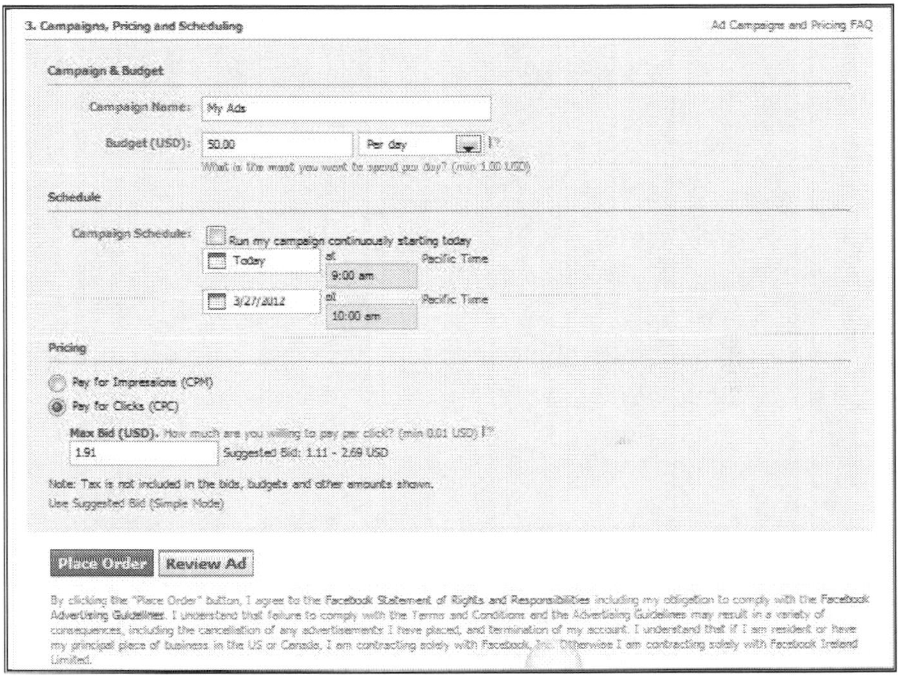

Figure 51: Facebook Ad Pricing and Scheduling

Determine your budget. You can choose a budget per day or for the life of the ad. The impressions will be displayed until your budget is reached. So, if you set a small daily budget, and it is reached by 9am, then no more impressions will be displayed until the next day. Similarly, if you are planning on running the ad for a week, and your lifetime budget is reached the second day the ad runs, then the impressions will no longer be displayed. Check on your ad periodically each day, and if you are meeting your budget early, then congratulate yourself on creating an enticing ad and consider raising your budget to take advantage of the activity and interest.

You are able to specify your ad's schedule or have it run continuously until you specifically stop the ad. If you uncheck this box, you are able to give a start and stop date and time.

In the "Pricing" section, you can choose between Pay-for-Impression or Pay-per-Click and specify what you are willing to bid. Notice the price difference. A Pay-per-Click ad bid may cost 25% or more that the Pay-for-Impression ad. However, with Pay-for-Impression, you are paying for each time the ad is displayed. Depending on your targeting, your ad may have 10,000+ impressions in a single day. Think about all of the computers out there with the Facebook site up while the user is away from their desk! Or the times that your ad is displayed a split second before a user changes screens. You are paying for all of those impressions that no one sees.

Using Pay-per-Click gives you the advantage of the nudge effect, but you only pay with someone actually clicks through.

Unlike traditional advertising, where you pay a specific amount of money for a specific amount of space in a magazine or newspaper in a specific section, or for a specific amount of time on a specific TV or radio station at a specific time of day, Facebook calculates a suggested bid range. There is only so much space on a Facebook User's Wall, so Facebook will use that space to advertise those ads with the highest bid. If your bid is in the lower range, you will likely get fewer impressions, and hence, fewer clicks. If you bid in the higher range, you may not have to pay the full bid amount, but you will outbid other advertisers and get more impressions, and hence, more clicks.

You can choose to "Use Suggested Bid", or click on that option and choose your own bid amount.

9.4 Review Ad and Place Order

Before you click on "Place Order", be sure to review your ad (Figure 52). Check the clarity of the image and check for misspelled or inaccurate words. Is the targeting you chose appropriate for the audience you want to reach? Double check that you have specified the correct bid amount, budget and duration. It is easier to go back and edit an incorrect ad from this point than it is after the ad is already running and seen by countless Facebook Users.

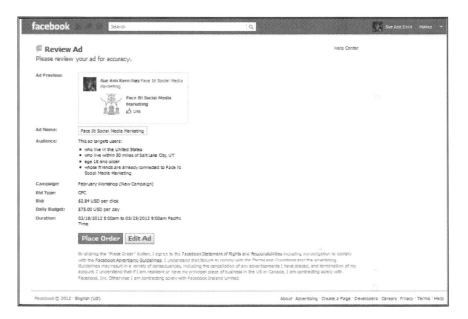

Figure 52: Review Your Ad

Once you had clicked on "Place Order", Facebook will review your ad and either OK or deny the ad. It has rarely taken me more than a few hours to get an email approval or denial. If you do get a denial, check for extensive use of capitalization or exclamation points. Are your photo and wording appropriate?

9.5   Viewing Your Facebook Ads

Facebook has created a dashboard allowing you to view your existing and ads. Scroll to the bottom of any screen and click on "Advertising". Your screen will show a chart of all of the campaigns you have run for all of the Pages you manage. You can click on the column headings to change the view the chart.

You can click on the specific ad to see how it was displayed, your target audience, and how much you paid.

You are also able to view all currently running ads and their performance. From this dashboard, you are able to change the name of the ad, change the duration, and even pause or delete the ad. This information is helpful as you create new ad campaigns.

The performance metrics given are similar to those given in Insights. How many impressions are you getting for the bid you gave? How many users have clicked through? Play around with the ad and change various parameters to see if your metrics improve.

10.0 Social Media Policy Guidelines

A social media policy guideline has becomes as important as an employee handbook or policy manual in today's business culture. Whether you have one employee or 10,000, it is necessary to clearly and comprehensively define acceptable usage of social media with regards to your business and your employees.

Inappropriate behavior on social media sites can adversely affect your business just as it can in the workplace. However, social media extends far beyond the walls of your business and the hours of operation. Chances are, many, if not most, of your employees are on Facebook or some other social media site.

Not only do you need to have a clear set of guidelines as to what is appropriate for your corporate social media presence, you must also let your staff understand what is acceptable behavior on their personal social media sites when it pertains to your business.

A post from a disgruntled employee is an obvious concern, but a seemingly innocent comment from a staff member on their Facebook Personal Profile could also have far reaching implications. Diligently respecting client confidentiality must be a high priority. Having a thorough written policy in place helps your employees understand how to properly interact online and how their behavior affects the company, their clients, vendors and business partners.

Consider these points when developing the guidelines for your social media policy. There are also many companies who have posted their social media guidelines on the internet, so feel free to do some searches and see what you can find to help you craft your policy.

10.1   Who Has Authority?

Determine who on your staff will have the responsibility and authority to maintain your social media sites. Will you allow all of your staff to post on your Page, or will you create a team whose responsibility it is to maintain the sites? Will you have everyone who posts on your Page be an Admin, or will you allow your staff to post from their Personal Profiles?

If you have several Admins, consider having them sign each of their posts with their first name. This adds a personal touch to the site and let's your Fans know that there is truly an individual behind the post, not just another "corporate suit".

The Manage Admin tool allows you to add and delete Admins for the Page. However, Facebook does not have a hierarchy of Admins that creates a primary Admin, Page Owner, or the like. Every Admin can delete every other Admin, so you will want to consider this when naming Admins. This is an oversight with Facebook and hopefully will be addressed soon. You will want to consider this when letting a current Admin go, to try and prevent them from hijacking the Page. Limit the number of Admins you allow on your Page and be sure you trust them!

10.2   How Much Time Is Allowed On Social Media Sites?

Chances are, your employees are participating on social media. Employees inherently find ways to waste time at work, and having access to the internet in general, and social media in particular, can add to this problem. However, allowing your staff access to your social media sites to monitor and participate in conversations can be a very productive part of their day. Rather than banning social media altogether, consider how much time you will allow your employees to participate. This may differ depending on their job duties, but may turn out to be as important as time set aside for networking and cold calling.

10.3   Who Handles Complaints?

If you find a negative comment from a Fan, how will you respond? Have in place a standard procedure so that the complaint or comment is elevated to the appropriate person, just as you would if you received the complaint in a phone call or letter.

In the social media world, it is often in your best interest *not* to delete the negative comment. Chances are, others have already seen the post and may have already made a comment themselves. The most effective reaction is to immediately respond to the post in a sincere and apologetic tone and offer to do whatever you can to look into and remedy the situation. Once you uncover and address a complaint, connect with the person publicly and then try to take the conversation off line.

Now do it! When you are taking actions to remedy a situation and doing what you can to satisfy the disgruntled customer, other will take note and respect your efforts. Often, taking care of a customer complaint quickly and effectively will turn that customer into a brand advocate who will share their story with their friends and create new sales opportunities for your business.

You may receive an unacceptable, disrespectful or inappropriate post on your Page that is not a customer service type issue. Likewise, you may encounter spam posts from Fans with the sole intention of posting information about their products, services, or money that you are about to inherit from a long lost royal relative in Nigeria. You can delete the post, ban the user from becoming a Fan on your Page in the future, and even report this user to Facebook.

10.4   Separate Business and Personal Profiles

As discussed earlier, Facebook does not allow anyone to use a Personal Profile to promote a business. And why would you want to? As shown, Facebook Pages have fabulous marketing tools that are not available to Personal Profiles. You may very well have friends who are also business associates or customers, and that is fine, but that will not always be the case. Chances are, you will have business associates with whom you are not friends and you don't want them to know what goes on in your personal life.

Post about your vacation, dog's latest tricks, or your bicycle ride this weekend on your Personal Profile and share that with your Facebook Friends. Post about your upcoming seminar, latest blog post, or interesting link to an intriguing news article on your business Page. By all means, share the post from your Page to your Personal Profile, but don't share your family reunion pictures on your business's Page!

We talked about how you can let your Fans know that you are the Admin of the Page in Section 5.4.5 if you choose not to be anonymous. This is a simple way to connect your business with your personal social media presence if you so desire.

10.5   Give Credit Where Credit Is Due

The web is a wealth of information. And honestly, how much information out there is truly unique? When posting information that was gleaned from another source, be diligent about citing that source. This also helps further the cause of the originator of the information, and they may appreciate your support in helping disseminate their information.

Likewise, be diligent in recognizing and complying with copyrights, patents, and trademarks.

10.6   Do Not Divulge Proprietary Information

It may seem obvious that your staff understands what corporate information is for public knowledge, and what is not. But what about your clients, venders, and other business associates? As tempting as it may be to post about the meeting with the long sought after client, or the big deal you just landed, this may not be information that should be shared. Be clear in your policy what information is to be kept confidential and what is acceptable to share.

10.7   Reputation Monitoring

Conversations about your company can happen anywhere on the web, whether or not you know about them. Wouldn't you like to know? Wouldn't you like to be able to respond to *positive* comments and compliments? Wouldn't you like to be able to respond to *negative* comments and complaints? Wouldn't you like to know what is being said about your *competition*?

It is important to search the web and social media channels regularly for mentions of your company so that you know what is being said and can determine the best way to respond. Listening and responding to these conversations will help you and your staff quickly address harmful and destruction situations and also give you a perspective to help you understand how your brand is seen in the industry.

Many monitoring tools exist to help you find mentions of key words and phrases relating to your business, competitors and industry. Many are free, yet, depending on your business, you may want to consider paid-or enterprise solutions.

Following is a list of a few of the many tools available for you to evaluate:

- Google Alerts (http://www.google.com/alerts)
- Google Blog Search (http://blogsearch.google.com)
- Twitter Search (http://search.twitter.com/)
- SiteVolume (http://www.sitevolume.com/)
- SocialMention (http://www.socialmention.com/)
- SocialCast (http://socialcast.com/)
- Enterprise-class solutions: Omniture, Radian6, Techrigy

10.8   Transparency and Disclosure

It goes without saying that businesses need to act ethically and truthfully with their customers. This is even more critical knowing that social media allows the masses to immediately react to a situation where they feel like they have been dealt with dishonestly. If it is found that you posted misleading or dishonest information on your site, it could blow up into a huge media frenzy.

Take, for example, the huge public relations debacle a few years ago when Wal-Mart hired bloggers Laura and Jim to write about their visits to various WalMarts during their cross-country RV trip. Wal-Mart did not disclose that they were paying Laura and Jim for their blogging, and instead led the public to believe that these were just regular folks who were big fans of the stores. When the ruse was exposed, it became a public relations firestorm for both Wal-Mart and the PR firm that created the blog and hired the bloggers.

If you are paying or giving free products or services to social media influencers for posting on your Page and promoting your business, you must disclose this relationship to the public. Not only is this the ethical thing to do, it is also the law.

11.0 Go Forth and Be Social!

Participating in social media can feel overwhelming. Don't we have enough responsibilities with our business? Where will I find the time?

There are thousands of social media sites out there with something advantageous about every single one. Don't feel like you have to participate in several of these in order to have a presence. It is impossible to be effective on more than a few sites simultaneously. At some point, you will be all "media" and no "social". However, with Facebook claiming more than 800 Million (that's an 8 with 8 zeros) users, it is critical to have a presence on this site and to take advantage of its popularity.

Don't let yourself get sucked in! Make the effort to build your Page completely and understand how to use it. Make time in your schedule to check Facebook for a few minutes each day, or a few times a week. Respond to your Fans' comments and post something creative, interesting and engaging. Check your reputation monitoring sites and respond appropriately and quickly. Then get off and do what you need to do to run your business.

Most importantly, have fun with social media! There is no other means of communication that allows you to interact with and create relationships with so many people in your neighborhood and around the world.

Let social media cause a fundamental change in the way you communicate!

12.0 Common Facebook Definitions

Activity Log   A streamlined list of all posts on a Page, including hidden posts, found Manage section of the Admin Panel.

Admin   A Facebook User that has editing and management capabilities for a Group or Page. A Face book user can be an Admin for an unlimited number of Pages, and a Page can have an unlimited number of Admins. (Short for administrator.)

Affinity   One of the three terms in determining EdgeRank. Affinity is the level of interaction between one Facebook User and another Facebook User or Page.

App   A program created by Facebook or by a 3rd party developer that expands the capability of the Facebook Personal Profile or Page and promotes interaction and conversation with other users.   (Short for application.)

Business Page The entity within Facebook that allows a Page to be created without being hosted by a Personal Profile. Business Pages do not have the same functionality and features of a Page that is hosted by a Personal Profile.

Comment   A message appended to an existing Facebook post.

Composer   The Facebook mechanism for posting status updates, photos, videos, links, questions and milestones

Cost Per Click The cost for having a user click through an ad to the destination Page or URL. Nothing charged for displaying the ad.

Cost Per Impression   The cost for displaying an ad 1000 times (CPM = Cost Per 1000 Impressions). This cost is charged regardless of whether or not a user clicks on the ad.

Cover Photo   The large image displayed on the Wall of a Facebook Page or Personal Profile to draw interest. The image must be at least 851 x 315 pixels. Facebook has strict guidelines for Page Cover Photos.

Edge Weight   One of the three terms in determining EdgeRank. Edge Weight is the level of importance of a post as shown by the addition of a photo, link, video, or question/poll.

EdgeRank   A proprietary algorithm, based on Affinity, Edge Weight, and Recency, or Time Decay, used by Facebook to determine what posts are shown in users News Feeds.

Fan   A Facebook Users who clicks on the "Like" button for a Page and has therefore given permission for that Page to post updates on the user's News Feed.

Friend   (noun) A Facebook User who has accepted a request to connect with another Facebook User.

(verb) To accept a Facebook User's request to connect.

Group   An entity within Facebook which allows users with a common interest to connect and communicate.

Highlighting   A tool for adding visibility to a post by increasing the width to the entire width of the Page Wall.

Home Page   The Home Page, or News Feed, on a Page or Personal Profile that shows a continuously updated list of posts by the user's Friends and Pages that they Like. The News Feed on the Personal Profile shows the updates posted by Friends and Pages that the user Likes. The News Feed on a Page shows the updates posts by other Pages that the Page Likes.

Impressions The number of times a post or Facebook Ad is displayed on a user's Wall.

Insights A free tool created by Facebook that generates data concerning Fan interaction for Page Admins to evaluate a Page's effectiveness.

Like (verb) To click on the "Like" button on a Page, thereby giving permission for that Page to post updates on your News Feed. Also, to click on to show support and agreement with post.

Likes (noun) The number of Facebook Users who are Fans of a Page.

Milestone A tool for creating a post that is meant for drawing attention a special date or occasion to a post on the Page Wall.

News Feed See Home Page

Page The entity within Facebook that allows an official and professional representation for a local business, place, company, organization institution, brand, product artist, band, public figure, entertainment, causes, or community entity to share information and interact with Facebook Users.

Pay-per-Click The means of paying for a Facebook ad whereby the Page is charged only when a user clicks on the ad

Pay-per-Impression The means of paying for a Facebook ad whereby the Page is charged each time an impression is displayed on a user's Wall.

Personal Profile The entity within Facebook that allows an individual to share information and interact with other Facebook Users.

Pinning A tool for creating visibility for a post by anchoring it to the top of the Page Wall for seven days and adding an orange flag for attention.

Post   (noun) The message created and uploaded onto a Facebook Page, Group or Personal Profile. Also known as an update.

(verb) The act of creating and uploading a message onto a Facebook Page, Group, or Personal Profile. Also known as an update.

Profile   The continuously updated collection of posts by a Facebook User or Page, along with any communication that is posted directly to the user or Page or on their comments. The Profile, or Wall shows only the posts made by the Page or user and any direct interactions with that Page or user.

Profile Picture   The image shown on the Page Wall that is used to help identify the Page to other Facebook Users. The Profile Picture can be up to 180 x 180 pixels, but will be cropped to 32 x 32 pixels for the Thumbnail

Recency   One of the three terms in determining EdgeRank referring to the amount of time elapsed since a post was created. The more recently a post was created, the higher the Recency score.

Reputation Monitoring Searching the web for mentions of a name, the name of a business, competitors, and other keywords to determine any mentions on social channels.

Share   The act of having a post from another Page or Friend's Wall copied onto your own Wall. You can also share an article or a link from outside of Facebook if the website has a Share button.

Thumbnail   The 50 by 50 pixel cropped version of the Profile Picture that is linked to the Page Posts and shown in Facebook Search

Time-Decay   See Recency

TimeLine   The series of post in chronological order on the Page Wall.

Update   See Post

User   An individual who has created a Facebook account.

Username   A custom URL created by an individual or a Page Admin that can be used to direct others to the Facebook Personal Profile or Page. Also known as a Vanity URL.

Vanity URL   See Username

Wall   See Profile

About the Author

Sue Ann Kern earned her Electrical Engineering degree during the time when computer generated graphics and desktop computing were in their infancy. The term "website" had not yet been used and the word "internet" did not yet exist. Believe it or not, it really wasn't that long ago!

Her early career as a digital designer and programmer led her to technical sales support and gave her opportunities to work with a wide range of dynamic companies. She kept her technical edge during the several years when she managed a tri-state, cosmetic dermatology practice. Her technical background blended with her business management experience has led her to embrace Social Media, which is a perfect mix of business and technology.

 www.facebook.com/FaceItSocialMedia

 www.linkedin.com/in/SueAnnKern

 @SueAnnKern

Made in the USA
Charleston, SC
20 April 2012